Buddhism and Buddhists in China

Lewis Hodus

This book has been published by:

Contact: sales@nuvisionpublications.com

URL: http://www.nuvisionpublications.com

Publishing Date: 2006

ISBN# 1-59547-958-9

Please see my website for several books created for
education, research and entertainment.

Specializing in rare, out-of-print books still in demand.

Table of Contents

PREFACE

This volume is the third to be published of a series on "The World's Living Religions," projected in 1920 by the Board of Missionary Preparation of the Foreign Missions Conference of North America. The series seeks to introduce Western readers to the real religious life of each great national area of the non-Christian world.

Buddhism is a religion which must be viewed from many angles. Its original form, as preached by Gautama in India and developed in the early years succeeding, and as embodied in the sacred literature of early Buddhism, is not representative of the actual Buddhism of any land today. The faithful student of Buddhist literature would be as far removed from understanding the working activities of a busy center of Buddhism in Burmah, Tibet or China today as a student of patristic literature would be from appreciating the Christian life of London or New York City.

Moreover Buddhism, like Christianity, has been affected by national conditions. It has developed at least three markedly different types, requiring, therefore, as many distinct volumes of this series for its fair interpretation and presentation. The volume on the Buddhism of Southern Asia by Professor Kenneth J. Saunders was published in May, 1923; this volume on the Buddhism of China by Professor Hodous will be the second to appear; a third on the Buddhism of Japan, to be written by Dr. R. C. Armstrong, will be published in 1924. Each of these is needed in order that the would be student of Buddhism as practiced in those countries should be given a true, impressive and friendly picture of what he will meet.

A missionary no less than a professional student of Buddhism needs to approach that religion with a real appreciation of what it aims to do for its people and does do. No one can come into contact with the best that Buddhism offers without being impressed by its serenity, assurance and power.

Professor Hodous has written this volume on Buddhism in China out of the ripe experience and continuing studies of sixteen years of missionary service in Foochow, the chief city of Fukien Province, China, one of the important centers of Buddhism. His local studies were supplemented by the results of broader research and study in northern China. No other available writer on the subject has gone so far as he in reproducing the actual thinking of a trained Buddhist mind in regard to the fundamentals of religion. At the same time he has taken pains to exhibit and to interpret the religious life of the peasant as affected by

Buddhism. He has sought to be absolutely fair to Buddhism, but still to express his own conviction that the best that is in Buddhism is given far more adequate expression in Christianity.

The purpose of each volume in this series is impressionistic rather than definitely educational. They are not textbooks for the formal study of Buddhism, but introductions to its study. They aim to kindle interest and to direct the activity of the awakened student along sound lines. For further study each volume amply provides through directions and literature in the appendices. It seeks to help the student to discriminate, to think in terms of a devotee of Buddhism when he compares that religion with Christianity. It assumes, however, that Christianity is the broader and deeper revelation of God and the world of today.

Buddhism in China undoubtedly includes among its adherents many high-minded, devout, and earnest souls who live an idealistic life. Christianity ought to make a strong appeal to such minds, taking from them none of the joy or assurance or devotion which they possess, but promoting a deeper, better balanced interpretation of the active world, a nobler conception of God, a stronger sense of sinfulness and need, and a truer idea of the full meaning of incarnation and revelation.

It is our hope that this fresh contribution to the understanding of Buddhism as it is today may be found helpful to readers everywhere.

The Editors.

New York city, December, 1923.

The Committee of Reference and Counsel of the Foreign Missions Conference of North America has authorized the publication of this series. The author of each volume is alone responsible for the opinions expressed, unless otherwise stated.

I. INTRODUCTORY

A well known missionary of Peking, China, was invited one day by a Buddhist acquaintance to attend the ceremony of initiation for a class of one hundred and eighty priests and some twenty laity who had been undergoing preparatory instruction at the stately and important Buddhist monastery. The beautiful courts of the temple were filled by a throng of invited guests and spectators, waiting to watch the impressive procession of candidates, acolytes, attendants and high officials, all in their appropriate vestments. No outsider was privileged to witness the solemn taking by each candidate for the priesthood of the vow to "keep the Ten Laws," followed by the indelible branding of his scalp, truly a "baptism of fire." Less private was the initiation of the lay brethren and sisters, more lightly branded on the right wrist, while all about intoned "Na Mah Pen Shih Shih Chia Mou Ni Fo." (I put my trust in my original Teacher, Saekyamuni, Buddha.)

The missionary was deeply impressed by the serenity and devotion of the worshipers and by the dignity and solemnity of the service. The last candidate to rise and receive the baptism of branding was a young married woman of refined appearance, attended by an elderly lady, evidently her mother, who watched with an expression of mingled devotion, insight and pride her daughter's initiation and welcomed her at the end of the process with radiant face, as a daughter, now, in a spiritual as well as a physical sense. At that moment an attendant, noting the keen interest of the missionary, said to him rather flippantly, "Would you not like to have your arm branded, too?" "I might," he replied, "just out of curiosity, but I could not receive the branding as a believer in the Buddha. I am a Christian believer. To be branded without inward faith would be an insult to your religion as well as treachery to my own, would it not? Is not real religion a matter of the heart?"

The old lady, who had overheard with evident disapproval the remark of the attendant, turned to the missionary at once and said, "Is that the way you Westerners, you Christians, speak of your faith? Is the reality of religion for you also an inward experience of the heart?" And with that began an interesting interchange of conversation, each party discovering that in the heart of the other was a genuine longing for God that overwhelmed all the artificial, material distinctions and the human devices through which men have limited to particular and exclusive paths their way of search, and drew these two pilgrims on the way toward God into a common and very real fellowship of the spirit.

A Buddhist monk was passing by a mission building in another city' of China when his attention was suddenly drawn to the Svastika and other Buddhist symbols which the architect had skilfully used in decorating the building. His face brightened as he said to his companion: "I did not know that Christians had any appreciation of beauty in their religion."

These incidents reveal aspects of the alchemy of the soul by which the real devotee of one religion perceives values which are dear to him in another religion. The good which he has attained in his old religion enables him to appropriate the better in the new religion. A converted monk, explaining his acceptance of Christianity, said: "I found in Jesus Christ the great Bodhisattva, my Saviour, who brings to fruition the aspirations awakened in me by Buddhism."

Just as it has been said that they do not know England who know England only, so it may be said with equal truth that they do not know Christianity who know it and no other faith. There are many in China like the old lady at the temple, who have found in Buddhism something of that spiritual satisfaction and stimulus which true Christianity affords, in fuller measure. The recognition of such religious values by the student or the missionary furnishes a sound foundation for the building of a truer spirituality among such devotees.

As will be seen in what follows, religion in China is at first sight a mixed affair. From the standpoint of cruder household superstitions an average Chinese family may be regarded as Taoists; the principles by which its members seek to guide their lives individually and socially may be called Confucian; their attitude of worship and their hopes for the future make them Buddhists. The student would not be far afield when he credits the religious aspirations of the Chinese today to Buddhism, regarding Confucianism as furnishing the ethical system to which they submit and Taoism as responsible for many superstitious practices. But the Buddhism found in China differs radically from that of Southern Asia, as will be made clear by the following sketch of its introduction into the Flowery Kingdom and its subsequent history.

II. THE ENTRANCE OF BUDDHISM INTO CHINA

Buddhism was not an indigenous religion of China. Its, founder was Gautama of India in the sixth century B.C. Some centuries later it found its way into China by way of central Asia. There is a tradition that as early as 142 B.C. Chang Ch'ien, an ambassador of the Chinese emperor, Wu Ti, visited the countries of central Asia, where he first learned about the new religion which was making such headway and reported concerning it to his master. A few years later the generals of Wu Ti captured a gold image of the Buddha which the emperor set up in his palace and worshiped, but he took no further steps.

According to Chinese historians Buddhism was officially recognized in China about 67 A.D. A few years before that date, the emperor, Ming-Ti, saw in a dream a large golden image with a halo hovering above his palace. His advisers, some of whom were no doubt already favorable to the new religion, interpreted the image of the dream to be that of Buddha, the great sage of India, who was inviting his adhesion. Following their advice the emperor sent an embassy to study into Buddhism. It brought back two Indian monks and a quantity of Buddhist classics. These were carried on a white horse and so the monastery which the emperor built for the monks and those who came after them was called the White Horse Monastery. Its tablet is said to have survived to this day.

This dream story is worth repeating because it goes to show that Buddhism was not only known at an early date, but was favored at the court of China. In fact, the same history which relates the dream contains the biography of an official who became an adherent of Buddhism a few years before the dream took place. This is not at all surprising, because an acquaintance with Buddhism was the inevitable concomitant of the military campaigning, the many embassies and the wide-ranging trade of those centuries. But the introduction of Buddhism into China was especially promoted by reason of the current policy of the Chinese government of moving conquered populations in countries west of China into China proper, The vanquished peoples brought their own religion along with them. At one time what is now the province of Shansi was populated in this way by the Hsiung-nu, many of whom were Buddhists.

The introduction and spread of Buddhism were hastened by the decline of Confucianism and Taoism. The Han dynasty (206 B. C.-221 A. D.) established a government founded on Confucianism. It reproduced the classics destroyed in the previous dynasty and encouraged their study; it established the state worship of Confucius; it based its laws and regulations upon the ideals and principles advocated by Confucius. The great increase of wealth and power under this dynasty led to a gradual deterioration in the character of the rulers and officials. The sigid Confucian regulations became burdensome to the people who ceased to respect their leaders. Confucianism lost its hold as the complete solution of the problems of life. At the same time Taoism had become a veritable jumble of meaningless and superstitious rites which served to support a horde of ignorant, selfish priests. The high religious ideals of the earlier Taoist mystics were abandoned for a search after the elixir of life during fruitless journeys to the isles of the Immortals which were supposed to be in the Eastern Sea.

At this juncture there arose in North China a sect of men called the Purists who advocated a return from the vagaries of Taoism and the irritating rules of Confucianism to the simple life practised by the Taoist mystics. When these thoughtful and earnest minded men came into contact with Buddhism they were captivated by it. It had all they were claiming for Taoist mysticism and more. They devoted their literary ability and religious fervor to the spreading of the new religion and its success was in no small measure due to their efforts. As a result of this early association the tenets of the two religions seemed so much alike that various emperors called assemblies of Buddhists and Taoists with the intention of effecting a union of the two religions into one. If the emperor was under the influence of Buddhism he tried to force all Taoists to become Buddhists. If he was favorable to Taoism he tried to make all Buddhists become Taoists.

But such mandates were as unsuccessful as other similar schemes have been. In the third century A. D. after the Han dynasty had ended, China was broken up into several small kingdoms which contended for supremacy, so that for about four hundred years the whole country was in a state of disunion. One of the strong dynasties of this period, the Northern Wei (386-535 A. D.), was distinctly loyal to Buddhism. During its continuance Buddhism prospered greatly. Although Chinese were not permitted to become monks until 335 A. D., still Buddhism made rapid advances and in the fourth century, when that restriction was removed, about nine-tenths of the people of northwestern China had become Buddhists. Since then Buddhism has been an established factor in Chinese life.

III. THE ESTABLISHMENT OF BUDDHISM AS THE PREDOMINATING RELIGION OF CHINA

Even the historical influences noted above do not account entirely for the spread of Buddhism in China. In order to understand this and the place which Buddhism occupies, we need to review briefly the different forms which religion takes in China and to note how Buddhism has related itself to them.

1. The World of Invisible Spirits

The Chinese believe in a surrounding-world of spirits, whose origin is exceedingly various. They touch life at every point. There are spirits which are guardians of the soil, tree spirits, mountain demons, fire gods, the spirits of animals, of mountains, of rivers, seas and stars, of the heavenly bodies and of many forms of active life. These spirits to the Chinese mind, of today are a projection, a sort of spiritual counterpart, of the many sided interests, practical or otherwise, of the groups and communities by whom they are worshipped. There are other spirits which mirror the ideals of the groups by which they are worshipped. Some of them may have been incarnated in the lives of great leaders. There are spirits which are mere animations, occasional spirits, associated with objects crossing the interests of men, but not constant enough to attain a definite, independent life as spiritual beings. Thus surrounding the average Chinese peasant there is a densely populated spirit world affecting in all kinds of ways his, daily existence. This other world is the background which must be kept in mind by one who would understand or attempt to guide Chinese religious experience. It is the basis on which all organized forms of religious activity are built. The nearest of these to his heart is the proper regard for his ancestors.

2. The Universal Sense of Ancestor Control

The ancestral control of family life occupies so large and important a place in Chinese thought and practice that ancestor worship has been called the original religion of the Chinese. It is certain that the earliest Confucian records recognize ancestor worship; but doubtless it antedated them, growing up out of the general religious consciousness of the people. The discussion of that origin in detail cannot be taken up here. It may be followed in the literature noted in the appendix or in the volume of this series entitled "Present-Day Confucianism." Ancestor worship is active today, however, because the Chinese as a people believe that these ancestors control in a very real way the good or evil fortunes of their descendants, because this recognition of ancestors furnishes a potent means of promoting family unity and social ethics, and, most of all, because a happy future life is supposed to be dependent upon descendants who will faithfully minister to the dead. Since each one desires such a future he is faithful in promoting the observance of the obligation. Consequently, ancestor worship, like the previously mentioned belief in the invisible spiritual world, underlies all other religious developments. No family is so obscure or poor that it does not submit to the ritual or discipline which is supposed to ensure the favor of the spirits belonging to the community. Likewise, every such family is loyal to the supposed needs of its deceased ancestors. In a very intimate way these beliefs are interwoven with the private and social morality of every family or group in Chinese society, and must be taken into account by any one who seeks to bring a religious message to the Chinese people.

3. Degenerate Taoism

Taoism is that system of Chinese religious thought and practice, beginning about the fifth century B. C., which was originally based on the teachings of Lao Tzu and developed in the writings of Lieh Tzu and Chuang Tzu and found in the Tao Te Ching. It is really in this original form a philosophy of some merit. According to its teaching the Tao is the great impersonal background of the world from which all things proceed as beams from the sun, and to which all beings return. In contrast to the present, transient, changing world the Tao is unchangeable and quiet. Originally the Taoists emphasized quiescence, a life in accordance with nature, as a means of assimilating themselves to the Tao, believing that in this way they would obtain length of days, eternal life and especially the power to become superior to natural conditions.

There is a movement today among Chinese scholars in favor of a return to this original highest form of Taoism. It appeals to them as a philosophy of life; an answer to its riddles. Among the masses of the people, however, Taoism manifests itself in a ritual of extreme superstition. It recommends magic tricks and curious superstitions as a means of prolonging life. It expresses itself very largely in these degrading practices which few Chinese will defend, but which are yet very commonly practiced.

4. The Organizing Value of Confucianism

Confucianism brought organization into these hazy conceptions of life and duty. It took for granted this spiritual-unspiritual background of animism, ancestor-worship and Taoism, but reshaped and adapted it as a whole so that it might fit into that proper organization of the state and nation which was one of its great objectives. Just as Confucianism related the family to the village, the village to the district, and the

14

district to the state, so it organized the spiritual world into a hierarchy with Shang Ti as its head. This hierarchy was developed along the lines of the organization mentioned above. Under Shang Ti were the five cosmic emperors, one for each of the four quarters and one for heaven above, under whom were the gods of the soil, the mountains, rivers, seas, stars, the sun and moon, the ancestors and the gods of special groups. Each of the deities in the various ranks had duties to those above and rights with reference to those below. These duties and rights, as they affected the individual, were not only expressed in law but were embodied in ceremony and music, in daily religious life and practice in such a way that each individual had reason to feel that he was a functioning agent in this grand Confucian universe. If any one failed to do his part, the whole universe would suffer. So thoroughly has this idea been adopted by the Chinese people that every one joins in forcing an individual, however reluctant or careless, to perform his part of each ceremony as it has been ordered from high antiquity.

The emperor alone worshipped the supreme deity, Shang Ti; the great officers of state, according to the dignity of their office, were related to subordinate gods and required to show them adequate respect and reverence. Confucius and a long line of noted men following him were semi-deified[1] and highly reverenced by the literati, the class from which the officers of state were as a rule obtained, in connection with their duties, and as an expression of their ideals. To the common people were left the ordinary local deities, while all classes, of course, each in its own fashion reverenced, cherished and obeyed their ancestors. It should be remarked at this point that Confucianism of this official character has broken down, not only under the impact of modern ideas, but under the longing of the Chinese for a universal deity. The people turn to Heaven and to the Pearly Emperor, the popular counterpart of Shang Ti.

Viewed from another angle, Confucianism is an elaborate system of ethics. In writings which are virtually the scriptures of the Chinese people Confucius and his successors have set forth the principles which should govern the life of a people who recognize this spiritual universe and system. These ethics have grown out of a long and, in some respects, a sound experience. Much can be said in their favor. The essential weaknesses of the Confucian system of ethics lie in its sectional and personal loyalties and its monarchical basis. The spirit of democracy is a deadly foe to Confucianism. Another element of weakness is its excessive dependence upon the past. Confucius reached ultimate wisdom by the study of the best that had been attained before his day. He looked backward rather than forward. Consequently a modern, broadly educated Confucianist finds himself in an anomalous position. He does not need absolutely to reject the wisdom which Confucianism embodies, but he can no longer accept it as a sound,

---

[1] Confucius was by imperial decree deified in 1908.

reliable and indisputable scheme of thought and action. Yet its simple ethical principles and its social relationships are basal in the lives of the vast masses of the Chinese.

5. Buddhism an. Inclusive Religion.

Upon this, confused jumble of spiritism, superstition, loyalty to ancestors and submission to a divine hierarchy Buddhism was superimposed. It quickly dominated all because of its superior excellence. The form of Buddhism which became established in China was not, to be sure, like the Buddhism preached by Gautama and his disciples, or like that form of Buddhism which had taken root in Burma or Ceylon. Except in name, the Buddhism of Southern Asia and the Buddhism which developed in China were virtually two distinct types of religion. The Buddhism of Burma and Ceylon was of the conservative Hinayana ("Little Vehicle" of salvation) school, while that of China was of the progressive Mahayana ("Great Vehicle" of salvation) school. Their differences are so marked as to be worthy of a careful statement.

The Hinayana, which is today the type of Buddhism in Ceylon, Burma and Siam, has always clung closely to tradition as expressed in the original Buddhist scriptures. Its basic ideas were that life is on the whole a time of suffering, that the cause of this sorrow is desire or ignorance, and that there is a possible deliverance from it. This deliverance or salvation is to be attained by following the eightfold path, namely, right knowledge, aspiration, speech, conduct, means of livelihood, endeavor, mindfulness and meditation. To the beatific state to be ultimately attained Gautama gave the name Nirvana, explained by his followers variously either as an utter extinction of personality or as a passionless peace, a general state of well-being free from all evil desire or clinging to life and released from the chain of transmigration. Hinayana Buddhism appeals to the individual as affording a way of escape from evil desire and its consequences by acquiring knowledge, by constant discipline, and by a devotedness of the life to religious ends through membership in the monastic order which Buddha established. It encourages, however, a personal salvation worked out by the individual alone.

The Mahayana school of Buddhists accept the general ideas of the Hinayana regarding life and salvation, but so change the spirit and objectives as to make Buddhism into what is virtually another religion. It does not confine salvation to the few who can retire from the world and give themselves wholly to good works, but opens Buddhahood to all. The "saint" of Hinayana Buddhism is the *arhat* who is intent on saving himself. The saint of Mahayana Buddhism is the candidate for Buddhahood (Bodhisattva) who defers his entrance into the bliss of deliverance in order to save others. Mahayana Buddhism is progressive. It encourages missionary enterprise and was a secret of the remarkable spread of Buddhism over Asia. Moreover, while the Hinayana school recognizes no god or being to whom worship is given, the Mahayana came to regard Gautama himself as a god and salvation as life in a heavenly world of pure souls. Thus the Mahayana type of thinking constitutes a bridge between Hinayana Buddhism and Christianity. In fact, a recent writer has declared that Hinayana Buddhists are verging toward these more spiritual conceptions. [2]

After the death of Sakyamuni[3] Buddhism broke up into a number of sects usually said to be eighteen in number. When Buddhism came to China some of these sects were introduced, but they assumed new forms in their Chinese environment. Besides the sects brought, from India the Chinese developed several strong sects of their own. Usually they speak of ten sects although the number is far larger, if the various subdivisions are included.

To indicate the manifold differences between these groups in Buddhism would take us far afield and would not be profitable. It will be of interest, however, to consider some of the chief sects. One of the sects introduced from India is the Pure Land or the Ching T'u which holds before the believer the "Western Paradise" gained through faith in Amitabha. Any one, no matter what his life may have been, may enter the Western Paradise by repeating the name of Amitabha. This sect is widespread in China. In Japan there are two branches of it known as the Nishi-Hongwanji and the Higashi-Hongwanji with their head monasteries in Kyoto. They are the most progressive sects in Japan and are carrying on missionary work in China, the Hawaiian Islands and in the United States.

Another strong sect is the Meditative sect or the Ch'an Men (Zen in Japan). This was introduced by Bodhidharma, or Tamo, who arrived in the capital of China in the year 520 A.D. On his arrival the emperor Wu Ti tried to impress the sage with his greatness saying: "We have built temples, multiplied the Scriptures, encouraged many to join the Order: is not there much merit in all this?" "None," was the blunt reply. "But what say the holy books? Do they not promise rewards for such deeds?" "There is nothing holy." "But you, yourself, are you not one of the holy ones?" "I don't know." "Who are you?" "I don't know." Thus introduced, the great man proceeded to open his missionary-labors by sitting down opposite a wall arid gazing at it for the next nine years. From this he has been called the "wall-gazer." He and his successors promulgated the doctrine that neither the scriptures, the ritual nor the organization, in fact nothing outward had any value in the attainment of enlightenment. They held that the heart of the universe is Buddha and that apart from

---

[2] See Saunders, *Buddhism and Buddhists in Southern Asia,* pp. 10, 20
[3] Sakyamuni is the name by which Gautama, the Buddha, is familiarly known in China.

17

the heart or the thought all is unreal. They thought themselves back into the universal Buddha and then found the Buddha heart in all nature. Thus they awakened the spirit which permeated nature, art and literature and made the whole world kin with the spirit of the Buddha.

"The golden light upon the sunkist peaks,
The water murmuring in the pebbly creeks,
Are Buddha. In the stillness, hark, he speaks!"[4]

Such pantheism and quietism often lead to a confusion in moral relations, but these mystics were quite correct in their morals because they checked up their mysticism with the moral system of the Buddha.

Still another important sect originated in the sixth century A. D. on Chinese soil, namely, the T'ien T'ai (Japanese Tendai), so called because it started in a monastery situated on the beautiful T'ien T'ai mountains south of Ningpo. Chih K'ai, the founder, realized that Buddhism contained a great mass of contradictory teachings and practice, all attributed to the Buddha. He sought for a harmonizing principle and found it in the arbitrary theory that these teachings were given to different people on five different occasions and hence the discrepancies. The practical message of this sect has been that all beings have the Buddha heart and that the Buddha loves all beings, so that all beings may attain salvation, which consists in the full realization of the Buddha heart latent in them.

There was a time when these sects were very active and flourishing in China. At the present time the various tendencies for which they stood have been adopted by Buddhism as a whole and the various sectaries, though still keeping the name of the sect, live peacefully in the same monastery. All the monasteries practice meditation, believe in the paradise of Amitabha, and are enjoying the ironic calm advocated by the T'ien T'ai. While the struggle among the sects of China has been followed by a calm which resembles stagnation, those in Japan are very active and the reader is referred to the volume of this series on Japanese Buddhism for further treatment of the subject.

When Buddhism entered China it brought with it a new world. It was new *practical* and new spiritually. It brought a knowledge unknown before regarding the heavenly bodies, regarding nature and regarding medicine, and a practice vastly above the realm of magical arts. In addition to these practical benefits, Buddhism proclaimed a new spiritual universe far more real and extensive than any of which the Chinese had dreamed, and peopled with spiritual beings having characteristics entirely novel. In comparison with this new universe or series of universes which Indian imagination had created, the Chinese universe

---

[4] K. J. Saunders in *Epochs of Buddhist History.*

was wooden and geometric. Since it was an organized system and a greater rather than a different one, the Chinese people readily accepted it and made it their own.

Buddhism not only enlarged the universe and gave the individual a range of opportunity hitherto unsuspected, but it introduced a scheme of religious practice, or rather several of them, enabling the individual devotee to attain a place in this spiritual universe through his own efforts. These "ways" of salvation were quite in harmony with Chinese ideas. They resembled what had already been a part of the national practice and so were readily adopted and adapted by the Chinese.

Buddhism rendered a great service to the Chinese through its new estimate of the individual. Ancient China scarcely recognized the individual. He was merged in the family and the clan. Taoists, to be sure, talked of "immortals" and Confucianism exhibited its typical personality, or "princely man," but these were thought of as supermen, as ideals. The classics of China had very little to say about the common people. The great common crowd was submerged. Buddhism, on the other hand, gave every individual a distinct place in the great wheel *dharma,* the law, and made it possible for him to reach the very highest goal of salvation. This introduced a genuinely new element into the social and family life of the Chinese people.

Buddhism was so markedly superior to any one of the four other methods of expressing the religious life, that it quickly won practical recognition as the real religion of China. Confucianism may be called the doctrine of the learned classes. It formulates their principles of life, but it is in no strict sense a popular religion. It is rather a state ritual, or a scheme of personal and social ethics. Taoism recognizes the immediate influence of the spirit world, but it ministers only to local ideals and needs. In the usages of family and community life, ancestor worship has a definite place, but an occasional one. Buddhism was able to leave untouched each of these expressions of Chinese personal and social life, and yet it went far beyond them in ministering to religious development. Its ideas of being, of moral responsibility and of religious relationships furnished a new psychology which with all its imperfections far surpassed that of the Chinese. Buddhism's organization was so satisfying and adaptable that not only was it taken over readily by the Chinese, but it has also persisted in China without marked changes since its introduction. Most of all it stressed personal salvation and promised an escape from the impersonal world of distress and hunger which surrounds the average Chinese into a heaven ruled by Amitabha [Footnote: Amitabha, meaning "infinite light," is the Sanskrit name of one of the Buddhas moat highly revered in China. The usual Chinese equivalent is Omi-To-Fo.] the Merciful. The obligations of Buddhism are very definite and universally recognized. It enforces high standards of living, but has added significance because it draws each devotee into a

19

sort of fellowship with the divine, and mates not this life alone, but this life plus a future life, the end of human activity. Buddhism, therefore, really expresses the deepest religious life of the people of China.

It will be worth while to note some illustrations of the conviction of the Chinese people that there are three religions to which they owe allegiance and yet that these are essentially one. They often say, "The three teachings are the whole teaching." An old scholar is reported to have remarked, "The three roads are different, but they lead to the same source." A common story reports that Confucius was asked in the other world about drinking wine, which Buddhists forbid but Taoists permit. Confucius replied: "If I do not drink I become a Buddha. If I drink I become an Immortal. Well, if there is wine, I shall drink; if there is none, I shall abstain." This expresses characteristically the Chinese habit of adaptation. Such a decision sounds quite up to date.

The Ethical Culture Society of Peking, recently organized, has upon its walls pictures of Buddha, Lao Tzu, Confucius and Christ. Its members claim to worship Shang Ti as the god of all religions. An offshoot of this society, the T'ung Shan She, associates the three founders very closely with Christ. It claims to have a deeper revelation of Christ than the Christians themselves. A new organization, the Tao Yuan, plans to harmonize the three old religions with Mohammedanism and Christianity.

Buddhism has consistently and continually striven to bring about a unity of religion in China by interpenetrating Confucianism and Taoism. Quite early the Buddhists invented the story that the Bodhisattva Ju T'ung was really Confucius incarnate. There was at one time a Buddhist temple to Confucius in the province of Shantung. The Buddhists also gave out the story that Bodhisattva Kas'yapa was the incarnation of Lao Tzu, the founder of Taoism. An artist painted Lao Tzu transformed into a Buddha, seated in a lotus bud with a halo about his head. In front of the Buddha was Confucius doing reverence. A Chinese scholar, asked for his opinion about the picture, said: "Buddha should be seated; Lao Tzu should be standing at the side looking askance at Buddha; and Confucius should be grovelling on the floor."

A monument dating from 543 A. D., illustrates this tendency of Buddhism to represent its own superiority in Chinese religious life. At the top of the monument is Brahma, lower down is Sakyamuni with his disciples, Ananda and Kas'yapa on one face, and on the other Sakyamuni again, conversing with Buddha Prabhutaratna and worshipped by monks and Bodhisattvas. On the pedestal are Confucian and Taoist deities, ten in number. Thus Buddhism sought to rank itself clearly above the other two religions. From the early days Buddhism regarded itself as their superior and began the processes of interpenetration and absorption. In consequence the values originally inherent in Buddhism have come to be regarded as the natural possession of the Chinese. It does express their religious life, especially in South China, where outward manifestations of religion are perhaps more marked than in the north.

IV. BUDDHISM AND THE PEASANT

In order that, one may realize the place that Buddhism holds in the religious life of the Chinese people as a whole, he must turn to the organizations through which it functions. It is sometimes difficult to estimate the place of Buddhism in China, because it so interpenetrates the whole cultural and social life of the people. It becomes their "way." To see how it touches the life of the average man or woman in various ways will, therefore, be illuminating. The most outstanding evidence of devotion are the many monasteries which dot the land in all Buddhist countries. China is less dominated by them than other lands, yet they form a very important reason for the persistence and strength of Buddhism there. One of the famous old shrines will represent them as a class and give evidence of their importance.

1. The Monastery of Kushan

Kushan Monastery, located about four hours' ride by sedan-chair from Foochow, is a famous shrine of South China. It occupies a large amphitheater about fifteen hundred feet above the plain, part way up Kushan, the "Drum Mountain," some three thousand feet high. From the top of the mountain on clear days with the help of a glass the blue shores of Formosa may be seen on the eastern horizon. The spacious monastery buildings are surrounded by a grove of noble trees, in which squirrels, pheasants, chipmunks and snakes enjoy an undisturbed life.

The ascent to the monastery begins on the bank of the Min River. At the foot of the mountain in a large temple the traveler may obtain mountain chairs carried by two or more coolies. The road, paved with granite slabs cut from the mountain side, consists of a series of stone stairs, which zig-zag up the mountain under the shadow of ancient pine trees. Every turn brings to view a bit of landscape carpeted with rice, or a distant view where mountains and sky meet. A brook rushes by the side of the road. Here it breaks into a beautiful waterfall. There it gurgles' in a deep ravine. The sides of the road are covered with large granite blocks which, loosened from the mountain side by earthquakes, have disposed themselves promiscuously. Their blackened, weather-beaten sides are incised with Chinese characters. One of them bears the words: "We put our trust in Amitabha." Another immortalizes the sentiments of some great official who has made the pilgrimage to the mountain. Near the monastery stand the sombre dagobas where repose the ashes of former abbots and monastery officials. Not far away on the other side of the road, hidden by trees, is the crematory where the last remains of the brethren are consumed by the flames.

23

As one approaches the monastery he hears the regular sounds of a bell tolled by a water-wheel, reminding the faithful of Buddha's law. He sees monks strolling leisurely about and lay brethren carrying wood, cultivating the gardens, or tending the animals released by pious devotees to heap up merit for themselves in the next world. Just inside the main gate is a large fish pond, where goldfish of great size struggle with one another, and with the lazy turtles, for the round hard cakes purchased from the monks by the merit-seeking devotee.

The monastery itself consists of a large group of buildings erected about stone-paved courts, rising in terraces on the mountain side. The large court at the entrance leads to the "Hall of the Four Kings." As one enters the spacious door, he *is* faced by a jolly, almost naked image of the "Laughing Buddha." This is Maitreya, the Mea siah of the Buddhists, who will return to the world five thousand years after the departure of Sakyamuni. In the northern monasteries Maitreya is often represented as reaching a height when standing of seventy feet or more, which indicates the stature to which man will attain when he returns to earth. On each side of the visitor are two immense images of the Deva kings. In Brahman cosmogony they were the guardians of the world. In this entrance hall of the Buddhist monastery they stand as guardians of the Buddhist faith. In the same hall looking toward the open court beyond is Wei To, another guardian deity of Buddhism. Somewhere near by is Kuan Ti, the god worshipped by the soldiers and merchants. Although a Confucian god, he was early adopted by Buddhist monks into their pantheon and made the guardian of their Order.

Beyond this entrance hall is a large stone-paved court. On the right side is a bell-tower whose bell is tolled by a monk who has kept the vow of silence for fourteen years. On the left is a drum-tower. On the right one finds a series of small shrines. A passage way leads to the library where numerous Buddhist writings repose in lacquered cases, some of them written in their own blood by devout monks. On the same side are guest halls, the dining room for three hundred monks, and the spacious, well equipped kitchen with running water piped from a reservoir in the hills above. A store where books, images and the simple requirements of the monks can be obtained is just above the dining room. On the left side of the court are large buildings used as dormitories far the monks, storerooms, and for housing the great printing establishment with its thousands of wooden blocks on which are carved passages from the Buddhist scriptures. Here also are kept the coffins in which the monks are to be burned.

On a terrace above the north side of the court rises the main hall, called the "Hall of the Triratna," the Buddhist Trinity, where three gilded images are seated on a lotus flower with halos covering their backs and heads. The center image is that of Sakyamuni, the Buddha. On his right is Yao Shih, the Buddha of medicine, and on the left, Amitabha. Quite often these images are said to represent the Buddha, the Law and the Community of Monks. On the altar are candlesticks and a fine incense burner from which curls of smoke arise. An immense lamp hangs from the ceiling. In the rear are banners with praises to Buddha given by pious devotees. The floor is tiled and covered with round mats made of palm fiber on which the monks kneel during worship. Before the mats are low stands for books. On each side of this main hall are the images of nine Buddhist saints (*arhats*), eighteen in all. Behind this large temple opens another court and on a terrace above it stands the hall of the Law with the images of Kuan Yin, the goddess of Mercy, and the twenty-four devas. Here also are small images of viceroys and patrons of the monastery.

The hillsides are dotted with numerous temples and shrines. There is one to Chu-Hsi, the great philosopher of the Sung dynasty, who was born in Fukien. In it are preserved a few characters indited by his hand. On the west side of the monastery are large buildings for the housing of animals released by merit-seeking devotees. Here cows, hogs, goats, chickens, geese and ducks spend their old age without fear of beginning their transmigration by forming the main portion of a Chinese feast.

The monastery is governed by an abbot, usually a man of good business ability, elected by the monks. Under him are the officers of the two wings or groups of attendants. One set looks after the spiritual interests, of the monks; the-other takes care of their material needs: The monks have worship about two o'clock in the morning and again at about four in the afternoon. The rest of the long day they spend in meditation, or study, in strolling about the mountain side or in sleep. Their life is separated from all stirring contact with the life of the world.

2. Monasteries Control Feng-shui

This monastery with its appointments is a good type of the monasteries all over China. It was founded at the request of the inhabitants of the neighborhood, because the dragons of the region used to cause much damage to the crops in the surrounding country. A holy monk came, founded the monastery, and by his good influence so curbed the dragons that the country-side has enjoyed peace ever since and the monastery has prospered. Since the fourth century of our era records show that by the building of monasteries in strategic place's holy monks brought rains and prosperity to various regions, or prevented floods and calamities from damaging the villages. In other words the monasteries are regarded as the controllers of *feng-shui* (wind and water). According to the Chinese philosophy winds and water are spiritual forces and may be so controlled by other spiritual forces that instead of bringing harm they will confer benefit upon the people. Floods and dry seasons are so frequent in China that any institution holding out the promise of regulating them would become firmly established in the affection of the people. The monasteries have taken this place.

One of the picturesque features of a Chinese landscape is the pagoda. These structures were introduced in the early stages of Buddhism to enshrine the relics of Buddha. It was said that Buddha's body consisted of eighty thousand parts, hence numerous pagodas were erected to shelter these relics. Inasmuch as a pagoda contained the relics of Buddha, it possessed magic power and so came to play a great part in the control of the winds and the rains. The pagoda in China has an odd number of stories varying from three to thirteen. The odd numbers belong to the positive principle in nature which is superior to the negative principle. The pagoda plays quite a part in the festivals of the people. On certain occasions the stories are hung with lanterns and the pagodas are visited by numerous throngs.

3. Prayer for Rain

Prayers for rain afford such a common illustration of the relation of Buddhism to the life of the peasant that a detailed presentation of such a service may be of seal value.

During a prolonged drought in some district of China, when the heat opens gaping cracks in the fields and the grain is drying up, the populace may visit their highest official and apprise him of the dire situation. He often forbids the slaughter of all animals for three days and, in case rain has not thereby come, he goes in person or sends a deputy to the nearest monastery to direct the monks to pray for rain.

(a) The Altar.—On such an occasion the great hall of the Law may be used for the ceremony. Quite often a special altar is erected in an enclosure near the monastery on a platform one foot high and twenty-five feet on each side, overspread by a tent of green cloth. In the center seats are arranged for the presiding monk and his assistants. On each of the four sides of the altar is placed an image of the Dragon King who is supposed to control the rain. If an image is not obtainable a piece of paper inscribed with the name of the dragon may be used. Flowers, fruits and incense are spread before the images. On the doors of the tent are painted dragons with clouds. The tent and altar are green and the monks wear green garments, because green belongs to the spring and suggests rain. For this ceremony the monks prepare themselves by abstinence and cleansing. The presiding monk is one of high moral character and religious fervor. While some monks recite appropriate sutras, two others look after the offerings, the incense, and the sprinkling of water during the ceremony to suggest the coming of rain. The services continue day and night, being conducted by groups of monks in succession.

(b) The Prayer Service.—The ceremonial is opened by a chant as follows:

"Pearly dew of the jade heavens, golden waves of Buddha's ocean, scatter the lotus flowers on a thousand thousand worlds of suffering, that the heart of mercy may wash away great calamity, that a drop may become a flood, that a drop may purify mountains and rivers.

"We put our trust in the Bodhisattvas and Mahasattvas that purify the earth."

The chant ended, a monk takes a bowl of water and repeats thrice: "We put our trust in the great merciful Kuan Yin Bodhisattva." Then follows the chant:

"The Bodhisattva's sweet dew of the willow is able to make one drop spread over the ten directions. It washes away the rank odors and dirt. It keeps the altars clean and pure. The mysterious words of the doctrine will be reverently repeated."

This chant ended, the monks intone incantations of Kuan Yin, quite unintelligible even to them, but of magical value. While these are being uttered, the presiding monk and his attendants walk around the altar, while one of them with a branch sprinkles water on the floor. This symbolizes the cleansing of the altar and of the monks from all impurities which might render the ritual ineffective. When the perambulating monks have returned to their place, while the sprinkler continues his duties, the monks repeat the words: "We put our trust in the sweet dew kings, Bodhisattvas and Mahasattvas."

The Bodhisattvas have now come to the purified altar and while the abbot offers incense to them, the monks repeat the words:

"The fields are destroyed so that they resemble the back of a tortoise. The demons of drought produce calamity. The dark people [Footnote: A term denoting the Chinese.] pray earnestly while crops are being destroyed. We pray that abundant, limpid liquid may descend to purify and refresh the whole world. The clouds of incense rise."

This plaint is repeated thrice and is followed by an invocation:

"Wholeheartedly we cast ourselves to the earth, O Triratna, who dost exist eternally in the realm of *dharma* of the ten directions."

The leader remains quiet a long time with his eyes closed, visualizing the Buddhas, the Bodhisattvas, the dragon kings, and the saints, all with their heavenly eyes and ears knowing that this region is afflicted

27

with drought, that an altar has been constructed and that all have come to make petition. This meditation is regarded as of chief importance. It is followed by an announcement to the effect that the sutra praying for rain was given by the Buddha, that a drought is afflicting the land, that the altar has been erected in accordance with the regulations and that prayer is being made for rain. But fearing that something may have been overlooked, the magic formula of "the king of light who turns the wheel" is read seven times so as to remedy such oversight.

The altar having thus been cleansed of all impurities, the rain sutra is opened and the one hundred and eighty-eight dragon kings are urged by name in groups of ten to take action. The formula is as follows:

"We with our whole heart invite such and such dragon kings to come. We desire that the heart and wisdom which knows others intuitively will move the spirits above to obey the Buddha, to take pity on the people below and to come to our province and send down sweet rain."

When the dragons have all been duly invited, the monks chant suitable magical formulas, while the leader sits in meditation visualizing these dragon kings and their tender solicitude for the people in distress. The monastery bell is sounded and the wooden fish is beaten, while drums and cymbals add their effect. The whole is intended to draw the attention of the dragon kings to the drought. Then the fifty-four Buddhas are invited in a similar manner in groups of ten, the sixth group consisting of four. A similar form of address is used and similar magical formulas are recited with the noisy accompaniment. The ceremony concludes by the expression of the hope that the three jewels (Buddha, the Law and the Community of Monks) and the dragon kings will grant the rain.

Upon the altar are four copies of an announcement to the dragon kings and Buddhas. On the first day three copies are sent to them through the flames, one to the Buddhas, one to the dragon kings and one to the devas. One copy is read daily and then sent up at the thanksgiving ceremony. The announcement is as follows:

"We put our trust in the limitless, reverent ocean clouds, the dragons of august virtue and all their host, all dragon kings and holy saints. Their august virtue is difficult to measure. In accord with the command of Buddha they send liquid rain. May their quiet mercy descend to the altar; may they send down purity and freshness, spreading over the ten directions. We put our trust in the company of dragon kings of the clouds, the saints and the Bodhisattvas."

The offerings are made only in the morning inasmuch as the Buddhas, following ancient custom, are not supposed to eat after the noonday meal. Great care is taken that the altar shall not be desecrated by any

28

one who eats meat or drinks wine. The magic formulas of great mercy are uttered or the name of Kuan Yin is repeated a thousand times. The monks, take turn in these services which continue day and night until rain comes.

(c) Its Meaning.—In the religious consciousness of the people is the idea that the drought is a punishment for sin. The altar is made pure and acceptable and sin is removed in various symbolic ways. This fits in with the idea that man is an intimate part of the world order. His sin disturbs the order of nature. Heaven manifests displeasures by sending down calamities upon men. Men should cease their wrongdoing which disturbs the natural order and should also wash away the effects of their sins. The services for rain with their magic formulas help to clear away the consequences of sin and to predispose Heaven to grant its blessings again.

4. Monasteries Are Supported Because They Control Feng-shui

The prayers for rain are an important part of the Chinese peasant's world order. Drought is the manifestation of Heaven's displeasure at the infraction of Heaven's laws. It calls for self-examination and repentance. Thus the monastery opens up the windows of the universal order as this touches the humble tiller of the soil.

The Buddhist monasteries not only hold services in time of drought, but also in time of flood and at times when plagues of grasshoppers afflict the land, or when diseases afflict human beings. Their adoption of Chinese customs led them to have special ceremonies at the eclipse of the sun and moon, although they knew the cause of the eclipse. Peasants and officials support the monastery because of these services regulating the wind and water influences and through them bringing the people into harmonious relation with the great world of spirits.

V. BUDDHISM AND THE FAMILY

One of the criticisms of the Chinese against Buddhism is that it is opposed to filial piety. According to Mencius the greatest unfilial act is to leave no progeny. In spite of this charge Buddhism has done much for the family. It has taken over the ethics of the family, filial piety, obedience and respect for elders, and has made them a part of its system. Transgression of these fundamental duties is visited by dire punishments in the next world. The faithful observance is followed not only by the rewards of the Confucian system, but results in the greatest rewards in the future life.

1. Kuan Yin, the Giver of Children and Protector of Women

Buddhism has done more. Out of its atmosphere of love and mercy toward all beings has developed Kuan Yin, the ideal of Chinese womanhood, the goddess of Mercy, who embodies the Chinese ideal of beauty, filial piety and compassion toward the weak and suffering. She is especially the goddess of women, being interested in all their affairs. Her image is found in almost every household and her temples have a place in every part of China.

A brief history of this deity will enable us to understand the significance of the cult. Kuan Yin started as a male god in India, called Avalokitesvara, who was worshipped from the third to the seventh century of our era. He was the protector of sailors and people in danger. In the course of time, either in China or in India, the god became a goddess. Some think that this was due to the influence of Christianity. In China both forms survive, though the goddess is better known. A Buddhist once said that a Bodhisattva is neither male nor female and appears in whatever form is convenient.

Kuan Yin is a very popular goddess. Her experiences in Hades are dramatically presented by traveling theatrical companies. Her deeds of mercy are portrayed in art. Her well known story runs as follows:

Kuan Yin was the daughter of the ruler of a prosperous kingdom located somewhere near the island of Sumatra. Her birth was announced to the queen by a dream. The little girl ate no meat nor milk. Her disposition was very good. Her intelligence was most extraordinary. Once she read anything she never forgot it.

At the age of sixteen her father tried to betroth her to a young prince. She refused and decided to give herself to a life of fasting and

31

abstinence. Angered b-v her obstinacy the father ordered her to take off her court dress and jewels, to put on the garb of a servant and to carry water for the garden. The garden never looked so beautiful. The daughter also looked well and showed no signs of weariness, because the gods assisted her in her work.

Relenting a little the king sent an older sister to urge Kuan Yin to accept the husband he had found for her. When she refused, he sent her to a monastery and charged the abbess to treat her harshly, so that she might be forced to return home. Expecting to win the king's favor, the abbess put the most unpleasant tasks on the girl. But again the gods assisted her and made her work light, so that her tasks were always well done and the young woman was cheerful.

One day the report came to the king that his daughter was associating with a young monk discussing heterodox doctrines and that she had given birth to a child. This news so enraged the king that he burned the monastery, killing many monks. The princess was captured and brought before him. Inasmuch as she was obdurate, the king ordered her to be executed. The executioner's sword, however, broke into a thousand pieces without doing her any injury. The king then ordered her to be strangled. A golden image sixteen feet high appeared on the spot. The princess laughed and cried: "Where there was no image, an image appeared. I see the real form. When body flesh is strangled, then appear the lights of ten thousand roads." She went to purgatory and purgatory at once changed into paradise. Yama, in order to save his purgatory, sent her back to the world. She appeared at Puto, an island off the coast of Chekiang near Ningpo. Here she rescued sailors and performed many miracles for people in distress.

In the meantime the father, who had committed many sins, became sick. His allotted time of life had been shortened by twenty years. Moreover, an ulcer grew on his body for every one of the five hundred monks he had killed when he burned the monastery. A miserable, loathsome old man, he came to an old monk, who was really the princess in disguise, and asked for help. The monk told him that an eye and an arm of a blood relative made into medicine was the only cure for his trouble. The two living daughters were willing to make such an offering, but their husbands would not permit them to do so. The old monk urged the monarch to take up a life of abstinence, to rebuild the monastery he had burned, and to provide money for services to take the five hundred monks whom he had killed through purgatory. He also said that a nun in the convent would offer an arm and an eye. When the monarch entered the monastery, he found hanging before the incense burner an arm and an eye. These were boiled, mixed with medicine and rubbed on the king's body. He soon became well. Further inquiry revealed that these members belonged to his daughter.

This is the story of the most popular goddess in China. She is worshipped by her devotees on the first and fifteenth of every month, on the nineteenth of the sixth month, when she became a Bodhisattva, and on the nineteenth of the ninth month, when she put on the necklace. A month after marriage every young bride is presented with an image of the Goddess of Mercy, an incense-burner and candlesticks.

This goddess is worshipped whenever trouble comes to man or woman. Her names signify her willingness to listen to all prayers. She is the "one who regards the voice," i.e., prayer; "one who hears the prayers of the world;" "one who regards and exists by himself as sovereign;" "the ancestor of Buddha who regards prayer;" "one who frees from fear;" "Buddha the august king;" "the great white robed scholar;" "great compassion and mercy."

2. Kuan Yin, the Model of Local Mother-Goddesses

This conception is the creation of the social and religious consciousness of the women in China. It reveals their aspirations for mercy, compassion, filial piety and for the beauty that crowns a well developed character. Such an ideal does not mean that these have been realized in all the numerous homes of the Chinese, but it manifests their sense of such an ideal to be realized in life and their ardent longing for its realization.

Mother-goddesses are found all over China and they have all of them been influenced by Kuan Yin. Some of them have originated with actual women who were deified after death. Here is the story of one of these goddesses who presides over the censer in a small temple in Formosa. She was born in the province of Kuangtung. At the age of seven she was adopted by a family as the future wife of their eighteen-year-old son. One day while crossing a river he was drowned. This was a great blow to her. When she was fourteen years old the father of the family died. The two women, thus left alone, wept bitterly day and night. The comfort of relatives was of little avail. The mother was becoming emaciated with grief. The daughter, unable to bear the strain any longer, washed herself, burned incense before the ancestral tablet of her betrothed, and then took this vow:

"I am willing to remain a virgin, to apply myself to carrying water and working at the mortar and to serve my mother-in-law. If I cherish any other purpose and change my chastity and obedience, may Heaven slay me and earth annihilate me."

When the mother heard this vow she stopped her weeping. Inasmuch as they had no uncle to look after them, they worked day and night. A relative of her future husband gave her one of his sons as an adopted son. The child died after a few months. This was a great grief. Then the mother died. The daughter sold her possessions to obtain money for a proper burial. She had only a coarse mourning cloth for her dress. After a while she adopted a child as her son. When he grew up she found him a wife who served her as faithfully as she had served her mother-in-law. When she was eighty years old, she dreamed that the golden maid and jade messenger of Kuan Yin stood beside her saying: "The court of Heaven has ordered you to become a god (shen)." She died soon after this. She said of herself:

"Shang Ti took compassion upon me during my life, because with a firm heart I kept my chastity and served my mother-in-law with complete obedience. Therefore he gave me the office of Kuan Pin. I have performed my duties in several places. Now I am transferred to Formosa."

This story and many others like it mirror the moral ideals of the women of China in the midst of their struggles for help and light and guidance.

3. Exhortations on Family Virtues

The Buddhists issue a large number of tracts. These are very commonly paid for by devotees who make a vow that, if their parent becomes well, they will pay for the printing of several hundred or thousand of these tracts for free distribution. In these tracts are usually many stories illustrating the rewards of filial piety. The story is told in one of them about a Mrs. Chin whose father-in-law being ill was unable to sleep for sixty days. His condition grew worse. Mrs. Chin knelt before Kuan Yin's altar, cut out a piece of flesh from her arm and cooked it with the father's food. His health at once improved and he lived to the age of seventy-seven. Another story is told in the same tract of a woman who cut out a piece of her liver and gave it as medicine to her mother-in-law.

These Buddhist tracts take up all the moral habits which make the family and clan strong and stable and surround them by the highest sanctions. A tract picked up in a Buddhist temple at Hangchow purports to be the revelation of the will of Buddha. It urges sixteen virtues. The first is filial piety. The tract says:

"Filial piety is the chief of all virtues. Heaven and Earth honor filial piety. There is no greater sin than to cherish unfilial thoughts. The spirits know the beginning of such thoughts. Heaven openly rewards a heart that is filial."

The second one mentioned is another important family virtue, namely, reverence:

"The saints, sages, immortals and Buddhas are the outgrowth of reverence. The greatest sin is to lack reverence for father and mother. When brothers lack reverence for one another, they harm the hands and feet. When husband and wife lack reverence, the harmony of the household is ruined. When friends do not have reverence, they bring about calamity."

Then follow similar exhortations on sincerity, justice, self-restraint, forbearance, benevolence, generosity, absence of pride, covetousness, lying, adultery, mutual love, self-denial, hope for the consolations of religion and for an undivided heart ruled by peace. These are virtues quite essential to the integrity of the family. They are taught, not in the abstract but by the exhibition of shining examples, by vivid representations of the rewards both here and hereafter, and by pictures of awful punishments. So by precept and example, by threat of punishment here and hereafter and by declaration of reward in the future Buddhism has tried to maintain the family virtues of the Confucian system and has attempted to permeate them by the spirit of sacrifice. Still it has always been the sacrifice of the weak for the strong, of the young for the aged, of the low for the high, of women for men.

4. Services for the Dead

Buddhism very early took over the relatively simple services for the dead and developed them into an elaborate ritual which made very vivid the spiritual universe which Buddhism introduced. In the sixth century a service was held in behalf of the father-in-law of Emperor Ning Ti (516-528 A. D.) for seven times every seven days. He feasted a thousand monks every day, and caused seven persons to become monks. On the hundredth day after the death he feasted ten thousand monks and caused twenty-seven persons to become monks.

Since that time services on every seventh day after the decease until the forty-ninth day, when a grand finale ends the ceremonies, have been very popular.

The object of such services is to conduct the soul of the dead through purgatory, in order that it may return to life or enter the Western Paradise. This is done by making a pleasing offering to the guardians and officers of purgatory, and to the gods and Bodhisattvas whose mercy saves people. Numerous missives are consigned to the flames, informing the rulers of the nether world about the soul of the dead; offerings of gold and silver, of various articles of apparel, of trunks, houses, and servants are made, all, however, made out of bamboo frames covered with paper. Various powerful incantations are recited which force open the gates of purgatory and let the soul out.

The services may be crowded into one day or they may be held on every seventh day until the forty-ninth day, i.e., seven sevens. Various explanations are given' for these services.

During the first week the soul of the dead arrives at the "Demon Gate Barrier." Here money is demanded by the demons on the ground that in his last transmigration the deceased borrowed money. Accordingly large quantities of silver shoes [Footnote: The silver used for this purpose is molded, in accordance with ancient usage, in the shape of shoes and carried about in that form by merchants.] must be sent to the dead so that he may settle all claims and avoid beating and inconvenience. During the second week the soul arrives at a place where he is weighed. If the evil outweighs the good, the soul is sawn asunder and ground to powder. In the third week he comes to the "Bad Dog" village. Here good people pass unharmed, but the evil are torn by the fierce beasts until the blood flows. In the fourth week the soul is confronted with a large mirror in which he sees his evil deeds and their consequences, seeing himself degraded in the next transmigration to a beast. In the fifth week the soul views the scenes in his own village.

In the sixth week he reaches the bridge which spans the "Inevitable River." This bridge is 100,000 feet high and one and three-tenths of an inch wide. It is crossed by riding astride as on a horse. Beneath rushes the whirl-pool filled with serpents darting their heads to and fro. At the foot of the bridge lictors force unwilling travelers to ascend. The good do not cross this bridge, but are led by "golden youth" to gold and silver bridges which cross the stream on either side of this "Bridge of Sighs."

In the seventh week the soul is taken first to Mrs. Wang who dispenses a drink which blots out all memories of the earthly life. Then the individual enters the great wheel of transmigration. This is divided into eighty-one sections from which one hundred and eight thousand small and tortuous paths radiate out into the four continents of the world. The soul is directed along one of these paths and is duly reborn in the world as an animal or as a human being or passes on into the Western Paradise.

In imitation of this bridge a bridge is built of tables in front of the home of the dead. At the end the tables are placed upside down and a lantern placed on each table-leg. At night this bridge is illuminated. A company of monks repeat their prayers and incantations, while others mount upon the bridge to impersonate devils. The pious son with the tablet of his deceased parent comes to take his father over the bridge. When his way is disputed by the demons, he falls on his knees and begs and gives them money, negotiating the passage at last with the aid of a large quantity of silver.

Another ceremony is the breaking through purgatory. Five supplications duly signed are addressed to the proper authorities, four being suspended at each of the four sides of the table and one at the center. Tiles are then placed over the table or on the ground. After incantations have been repeated to the accompaniment of the sounding of the bell and the wooden fish, the supplications are burned and the tiles are broken as a symbol of breaking through purgatory and of releasing the soul.

Thus Buddhism has taken over the most important function of ancestor worship, has extended it and made it more significant to each individual as well as to the family.

VI. BUDDHISM AND SOCIAL LIFE

1. How the Laity is Trained in Buddhist Ideas

A common way of emphasizing moral ideas among the people by Buddhist teachers is the use of tracts purporting to have a divine origin. The following gives the substance of such a tract:

Not long ago in the province of Shantung, there was a sharp and sudden clap of thunder. After the frightened people had collected their wits, they discovered a small book written in red in front of the house of a certain Mr. Li. Mr. Li picked up the book, copied it and read it reverently. He gave a copy to Mr. Ma, the prefect, but Mr. Ma did not believe in the book. Thereupon Maitreya, the Messiah of the Buddhists, spoke from the sky as follows:

"These are the years of the final age. The people under heaven do not reverence Heaven and Earth, they are not filial to father and mother, they do not respect their superiors. They cheat the fatherless, impose upon the widow, oppress the weak; they use large weights for themselves and small measures for others. They injure the good. They covet for their own profit. They cheat men of money, use the five grains carelessly, kill the cow that draws the plow. This volume is sent for their special benefit. If they recite it they will avoid trouble. If they disbelieve, the years with the cyclical character Ping and Ting will have fields without men to plant them and houses without men to live in them. In the fifth month of these years evil serpents will infest the whole country. In the eighth and ninth months the bodies of evil men will fill the land.

"Those who believe this book and propagate its teachings will not encounter the ten sorrows of the age: war, fire, no peace day and night, separation of man and wife, the scattering of the sons and daughters, evil men spread over the country, dead bones unburied, clothing with no one to wear it, rice with no one to eat it, and the difficulty of ever seeing a peaceful year. Sakyamuni foreseeing this final age sent down this volume in Shantung. The Goddess of Mercy saw the sorrows of all living beings.

39

Maitreya commanded the two runners of T'ai Shan, the god of the Eastern Mountain, to investigate the conduct of men and as a first punishment to increase the price of rice, and then besides the ten sorrows already mentioned above, to inflict the punishments of flood, fire, wind, thunder, tigers, snakes, sword, disease, famine and cold. The rule of Sakyamuni which has lasted twelve thousand years is now fulfilled, and Maitreya succeeds to his place."

These sorrows may be escaped by reciting this sutra whose substance we find above. If it is repeated three times the person will escape the calamity of fire and water. If one man passes it on to ten men and ten men pass it on to a hundred, they will escape the calamities of sword, disease and imprisonment, and receive blessings which cannot be measured. He who in addition to repeating the sutra practices abstinence will insure peace for himself. He who presents one hundred copies to others will insure his personal peace. He who presents a thousand copies will insure the peace of his family. He who is attacked by disease, may escape it by taking five cash of the reign of Shun Chih (1644-1661 A. D.), the first emperor of the Ch'ing dynasty, one mace of the seed of cypress, one mace of the bark of mulberry, boil in one bowl of water until only eight-tenths of the water remain, drink and he will become well.

In this way the five Buddhist commandments for the laity not to kill any living creature, not to steal, not to commit adultery, not to lie, and not to use intoxicating liquor are propagated and made real to the common man. The method is quite efficient. Whole provinces have been put into a panic by such prophecies.

2. Effect of Ideals of Mercy and Universal Love

The command not to kill any living being has had considerable influence in China. There are volumes of stories telling of the punishments which will be visited upon those who disobey and of the rewards of those who release living animals. Every monastery has a special place for animals thus released by pious devotees.

There is a popular story about a fishmonger of the T'ang dynasty who was taken sick and during his illness dreamed that he was taken to purgatory. His body was aflame with fire and pained him as though he were being roasted. Flying fiery chariots with darting flames swept around him and burned his body. Ten thousand fish strove with one another to get a bite of his flesh. The ruler of the lower regions accused him of killing many fish and hence his punishment. For a number of days he was hanging between life and death. His relatives were urged to perform some works of penance. They had his fishing implements

40

burned. With reverent hearts they made two images of Kuan Yin, presented offerings and repented. The whole family performed abstinence, stopped killing living things, printed and gave away over a hundred copies of the Diamond Sutra, and ferried over a large number of souls through purgatory. As a result of their efforts the sick man became well.

The following comment was made on the above story by a scholar. If its premises are granted, the conclusion is inevitable:

"If the fiery chariots are seal, why does not man see them? If they are false, how is it that man feels the pain? But where do the fiery chariots come from? They come from the heart and head of the one who kills fish. The fire in the heart (heart belongs to the element fire) causes destruction. The chariot fire also causes destruction."

This attitude of mercy has been extended to human beings. There are numerous tracts against the drowning of little girls in those regions where this custom is prevalent. One tells the following story:

In the province of Kwangtung there lived a Mrs. Chang who daily burned incense and repeated Buddha's name. One day she and her husband died. Much to their surprise and consternation Yama (the potentate of hell) decided that Mr. Chang must become a pig and Mrs. Chang a dog. Mrs. Chang accordingly went to Yama and said, "During life we honored Buddha and so why should we become animals after death?" Yama said, "What use is it to honor Buddha? During life you drowned three girls whom I sent into life. People with the face of a man and the heart of a beast, should they not be punished?" The husband accordingly took on a pig's skin and the wife a dog's. Then by a dream they revealed to their brother Chang number two that, although they repeated Buddha's name, they were not permitted to be reborn as men, because they had drowned little girls.

Perhaps the extent of this spirit, of mercy and its possibilities may be illustrated by the reverence for the ox. While there is a great deal of cruelty in China to animals and men, it is rarely that one sees an ox abused. Up to the advent of the foreigner an ox was not killed for meat. In many places in China today the slaughter of an ox would bring the punishments of the law upon the butcher. No doubt this reverence is due to the great Indian reverence for the cow. The law of kindness has been extended to other animals, taking the rather spectacular form of releasing a few decrepit animals and allowing them to spend their last days in a monastery compound. There are many kindly things done in China. The dead are buried, the sick are provided with medicine. Every year numerous wadded garments are given away to poor people. Various groups carrying on a humble ministry of helpfulness have found a real inspiration in the ideals held before them in Buddhism, the rewards promised and punishments threatened.

3. Relation to Confucian Ideals

Why have not these ideals exercised a larger influence in China? The answer is quite simple. The activities of the monks have been strenuously opposed by the Confucian state system. The philosopher, Chang Nan-hsiian, a contemporary of Chu-Hsi, states concisely for us the differences betwen Confucianism and Buddhism in his comment on a passage in the *Book of Records.*

"Strong drink is a thing intended to be-used in offering sacrifices and entertaining guests,—such employment of it is what Heaven has prescribed. But men by their abuse of such drink come to lose their virtue and destroy their persons—such employment of it is what Heaven has annexed its terrors to. The Buddhists, hating the use of things where Heaven sends down its terrors, put away as well the use of them which Heaven has prescribed.

"For instance, in the use of meats and drinks, there is such a thing as wildly abusing and destroying the creatures of Heaven. The Buddhists, disliking this, confine themselves to a vegetable diet, while we only abjure wild abuse and destruction. In the use of clothes, again, there is such a thing as wasteful extravagance. The Buddhists, disliking this, will have no clothes but those of a dark and sad color, while we only condemn extravagance. They, further, through dislike of criminal connection between the sexes, would abolish the relation between husband and wife, while we denounce only the criminal connection.

"The Buddhists, disliking the excesses to which the evil desires of men lead, would put away, along with them, the actions which are in accordance with the justice of heavenly principles, while we, the orthodox, put away the evil desires of men, whereupon what are called heavenly principles are the more brightly seen. Suppose the case of a stream of water. The Buddhists, through dislike of its being foul with mud, proceed to dam it up with earth. They do not consider that when the earth has dammed up the stream, the supply of water will be cut off. It is not so with us, the orthodox. We seek only to cleanse away the mud and sand, so that the pure water may be available for use. This is the difference between the Buddhists and the Learned School." [5]

This statement reveals at once the opposition of the sect of the Learned and the influence which Buddhism exerted upon its members.

---

[5] *Shu King,* Pt. V, Bk. X, p. 122.

Buddhism while enjoying occasional favor from the state was often zealously persecuted. In 819 Han Yii issued his celebrated act of accusation. In 845 the emperor Wu Tsung issued his decree of secularization. At that time 4600 monasteries and 40,000 smaller establishments were pulled down and 265,000 monks and nuns were sent back to lay life. Their rich lands were confiscated. Under the Ming dynasty, as well as under the Ch'ing dynasty, Buddhism enjoyed a precarious existence. Whether Buddhism would have improved the moral conditions of the Chinese; if it had been given a free hand, is difficult to affirm. Still its failure is at least partly due to the opposition of Confucian orthodoxy.

4. The Embodiment of Buddhist Ideals in the Vegetarian sects

The state persecutions of Buddhism forced it to leave temporarily its institutional life and trust itself to the people. These persecutions were usually followed by a revival of piety and religion among the people. The Buddhist teachers gathered about themselves a large number of lay devotees who formed societies which practice religious rites in secret. These sects have preserved the genuine Buddhist piety, not only in times of persecution, but at times when the Buddhist organization under imperial favor was departing from its simplicity.

A number of these sects have continued under different names for several centuries. For example, the Tsai Li, a society now enjoying a quiet existence in North China, is successor to the White Lotus society. The latter started in the fifth century. Its members sought salvation in the Pure Land of Amitabha. In the eleventh century it enjoyed imperial favor. During the Mongol dynasty it fought against the throne with rebels and placed one of its leaders, Chu Yuean-chang, a monk, on the throne, who became the founder of the Ming dynasty. The sect was soon proscribed and its members persecuted by the government. During the Ch'ing dynasty it took part in a rebellion and was ruthlessly exterminated. At present it goes under the name of *Tsai Li,* i.e., within the Li or principles of the three religions. It is a mediator among the three religions.

There are thirty-one organizations of this sect in Peking and branches throughout North China. The society forbids the use of wine and opium, though it does not forbid the use of meat. It usually has a Buddhist image, Kuan Yin or some other. It uses Buddhist prayers and incantations. The outstanding doctrines held during its long history have been the hope of salvation in the Western Heaven of Amitabha, the early coming of Maitreya, the Buddhist Messiah, and the large use of magic formulas and incantations.

Another sect which embodies Buddhist ideals is the Chin Tan, the sect of the philosopher's stone or pill of immortality. Its founder was the writer of the Nestorian tablet and so the sect is related to Christianity. It exalts the teaching of universal love. This is one of several examples of a supposed contact between Buddhism and Christianity.

These sects of which the two above are examples are present in all parts of China. They obey the five Buddhist commandments for laymen. The members spend much time in fasting and prayer, and in the repetition of Buddhist books. Their lives as a rule are simple and sincere. They are preparing for rebirth in the land of Amitabha, or are expecting the early coming of the Buddhist Messiah to set this world right. In the meantime, by means of incantations, personal regimen and cooperative action they are doing all they can to usher in a better state.

5. Pilgrimages

Pilgrimages are very popular in China. The famous Buddhist shrines are Wu T'ai Shan in Shansi, Puto on the coast of Chekiang, Chiu Hua Shan in Anhwei, and Omei Shan in Szechuan. These, one on each side of China, represent the four elements of Buddhist science, wind, water, fire and earth. They are also the centers of the worship of the four great Bodhisattvas, Wenshu, Kuan Yin, Titsang and Puhsien. Besides these large centers there are many others to which pilgrims direct their footsteps.

In the spring of the year, when the god of spring covers the earth with a green mantle, when the sky and winds call, many start on their pilgrimage. Many go singly and laboriously, kneeling and bowing every few steps. Others go in happy companies, chaperoned by a pious, village dame, who has organized the group. Some go because their turn has come. They are members of a guild which has a fund devoted to pilgrimages by its members. Some go for the performance of a vow made to Kuan Yin, when the father was sick unto death and the goddess prolonged his life. To others it is the culmination of a pious life. All go for the joy which travel in the spring gives.

Puto, an island off the coast of Chekiang, is the goal of many pilgrims from all parts of China. In, the monasteries on the island are about two thousand monks. In the pilgrim season this number is increased to ten thousand monks and thousands of lay pilgrims.

A group of pilgrims was going along merrily. The sun was bright, lighting up the white caps on the deep blue sea. Spring was rioting all about. One member was an abbot from Hangchow. A small, humble-looking man with a few straggling long hairs where the mustache usually grows, was a lay Buddhist from Wuchang. One was a bright young monk from Tientsin. Last, but almost omnipresent and always bubbling over, was a servant of the abbot from Hangchow. He was in the presence of divinity and his whole life was heightened for the time being. "Why did you come!" they were asked. "We came to worship the holy mother, Kuan Yin." When they entered a shrine each purchased three sticks, of incense and two candles and reverently placed them before the image of the goddess, kneeling and bowing. Then they sat and partook of the tea offered by the attendant. After paying a small gratuity, they went on to the next shrine.

On the way a large black snake as thick as an arm lazily crossed over the road. They stood, reverent and awestruck, until he disappeared in the grass, remarking that this was a good omen. When crossing a sand dune piled up by the winds the abbot from Hangchow remarked that this was called the flying sand, wafted there by the goddess who took pity on some travelers who had been compelled to cross a narrow strait in order to come to a cave. This cave, called Fan Yin Tung, is one of the rifts made by an earthquake and washed out by wind and waves. Below it rushes the tide; from above the sun sends down a few rays. Each pilgrim after offering incense looks into the darkness to see whether he can behold in the dark cavern an image of some Buddha. One sees Kuan Yin and is acclaimed as having had a good vision. Another sees the Laughing Buddha. All exclaim that he has been the most fortunate of all, for this Buddha is the Messiah to come and he who beholds him will be blessed. So from place to place they wander, chatting and seeing the sights of the island. Thus thousands are doing in various parts of China, and in this way strengthening the hold of Buddhism upon themselves and their communities.

VII. BUDDHISM AND THE FUTURE LIFE

Before the advent of Buddhism the Chinese had only a vague idea regarding life after death. The Land and Water Classic mentions the Tu Shuo mountain in the Eastern Sea, under which spirits of the dead live, the entrance guarded by two spirits, Shen Tu and Yue Lei, who are in general control of the demons. In some parts of China the names or pictures, of these spirits are placed on the doors of a house to guard it. The Taoists early developed the idea of a western paradise presided over by the Queen of the West, located at first in the K'un Lun mountains and later in the islands of the Eastern Sea. This heaven, however, was limited to Taoist hermits and mystics. Buddhism made a complete purgatory and heaven known to every one in China.

1. The Buddhist Purgatory

This is really Buddhism's most noteworthy addition to China's religious equipment; Buddhism lays much stress upon the experiences of a soul immediately after death. Its punishments are well known to every individual. The temple of the City Guardian found in every walled city has a replica of the court in purgatory over which he presides. In the temples of T'ai Shan there is an elaborate exhibit of the tortures inflicted on culprits in purgatory. Every funeral service conducted by Buddhists or Taoists is intended to conduct the soul of the dead through purgatory and pictures vividly the progressive experiences from the first seventh day to the seventh seventh day. On the the seventh month, on the fifteenth day [about August] a special service is held for the souls of the dead in purgatory. Furthermore, every community has a general service [about October] for the souls of those who died a violent death or who have no one to look after them. During the war many services were thus held for those who died on the battlefields of Europe. At such services the scenes in purgatory are vividly portrayed by pictures and figures. The temples distribute tracts with pictures of purgatory so that women may see them and understand. On the stage are often acted powerful plays whose scenes are laid in Hades. This propaganda is perhaps the most efficient of its kind.

Purgatory is depicted as consisting of ten courts each surrounded by small hells, where the soul undergoes punishment and cleansing. The fifth court, which may be taken as an example of the other courts, is in charge of Yen Lo or Yama. Yama was once in charge of the first court, but his tender heart pitied the souls who came before him and sent them back to earth. Because of this leniency he was placed in charge of the fifth court.

When a soul has passed through the first four courts and it has been discovered that there is no good conduct to its credit, it is led to the fifth court and examined every seven days regarding past conduct. In order to get back to the world of men, it eagerly promises to complete various unfinished vows, such as to repair monasteries, schools, bridges, or roads, to clean wells, to deepen rivers, to distribute good books, to release animals, to take care of aged parents, or to bury them suitably. But it is plainly told that the gods know its artifices, and that now these unfinished tasks can never be completed. The gods have reached the unanimous opinion that no injustice is being done. Accordingly there is no appeal, but each soul is led by attendants with bulls' heads and horses' faces to a tower whence they may see their native village. Its front is in the shape of a bow with a perimeter of twenty-seven miles; its height is four hundred and ninety feet. It is guarded by walls of sword trees.

Good men, whose deeds of omission are balanced by the good they have done, return to life. Only souls judged to be evil see their village from this tower. These can see their own families moving about, and can hear their conversation. They realize how they disobeyed the teachings of their elders. They see that the earthly goods for which they have struggled are of no value. Their plottings rise up with lurid reality. They see how they planned a new marriage although already married, how they appropriated fields, state property, and falsified accounts, putting the blame on persons who were dead. While they observe their village they behold their erstwhile friends touch their coffin and inwardly rejoice. They hear themselves called selfish and insincere. But their punishment does not stop here. They behold their children punished by magistrates, their women afflicted with strange diseases, their daughters ravished, their sons led astray, their property taken away, the ancestral house burned and their business ruined. From this tower all passes before them as a lurid dream and they are stricken in heart.

About the fifth court are sixteen small hells where the soul is punished. In each one are stakes buried in the ground and fierce animals. The hands and feet of the guilty one are bound to a stake, his body is opened with small knives, and his heart and intestines quickly devoured.

In each of these sixteen hells is a certain type of sinner: (1) Those who do not reverence the gods and demons and who doubt the existence of rewards and punishments; (2) those who hurt and kill living beings; (3) those who break their vows to do good; (4) those who resort to heterodox practices and vainly hope to attain eternal life; (5) those who upbraid good men, fear the wicked and hate men because they do not die speedily; (6) those who strive with other people and then put the blame upon them; (7) men who force women; and women

48

who seduce young men, and all who have libidinous desires; (8) those who gain profit for themselves by injuring others; (9) the stingy and those who absolutely disregard others, whether alive or dead, giving them no help in dire need, when they can do so without injury to themselves; (10) those who steal and put the crime upon others; (11) those who requite favors with hate; (12) those whose hearts are perverse and poisonous, who instigate others to do wrong even if they may not have carried out their suggestion; (13) those who tempt others by deceit; (14) those who involve others in their squabbles and in gambling and then themselves win out; (15) those who stubbornly persist in their false ideas, do not repent, and slander others; (16) those who hate good and virtuous men.

Besides these sixteen sorts of sinners the fifth court deals with other types of wicked people; those who do not believe in rewards and punishments after death, who hinder good causes, who burn incense without a sincere heart, speak of the sins of others, who burn books that urge men to be good and worship the Great Dipper, but persist in eating meat; those who hate men; who repeat sutras and incantations, and take part in religious ceremonies, but do not fast beforehand; who slander the Buddhist and Taoist religions; who know how to read, but refuse to read the ancient and modern exhortations regarding rewards and punishments; who dig into graves and destroy their marks, who purposely set fire to trees and underbrush, or are careless with fire in their own houses; who shoot arrows at animals with the intent, to kill; who urge and tempt the sick and weak to enter into contests of any kind with themselves; who throw tiles and stones over neighboring walls, poison fish in the river, fire guns, or make nets or traps for birds; who sow salt on the ground, who do not bury dead eats and snakes very deep and thus cause death to those who dig; who cause men to dig the frozen ground in winter or spring (the vapors of earth chill such diggers to death); who tear down adjoining walls and compel their neighbors to move the kitchen stove; who appropriate public highways, lands, close wells and stop gutters.

Those who have committed any of the above sins are taken, to the tower whence they can see their own village and then are consigned to the great crying hell, Raurava, that is, the fourth of the Buddhist hot hells. [Footnote: Buddhism distinguishes hot and cold hells. In a country like India severe cold is a serious torture.] Thence they go to their respective small hells. When their time has expired, they are examined in order to see whether they have any other sins which need punishment.

Those who have committed any of the above sins may not only escape punishment, but may have their punishment in the sixth court lessened, if they fast regularly on the eighth day of the first month and take a vow not to commit these sins. Some sins, however, cannot be arranged for in such a way, such as the killing of living beings and hurting them; the associating with heretics; committing fornication with women and then poisoning them; committing adultery, violence, envy, or injuring the good name of others; stealing, requiting favors with hatred, and hearing exhortation but not repenting. These are major sins.

2. Its Social Value

The social value of purgatory is quite plain from the description of the fifth court and of the sinners who are punished therein. Purgatory is the social mirror of China, wherein the consequences of all unsocial acts are pictured in such a vivid way as to deter the individual from committing them. It is effective in China, not only because of the realistic presentation, but because the opinion of the community is against such acts and in favor of repressing them on every occasion.

3. The Buddhist Heaven.

Buddhism brought into China not only a fully developed purgatory but also a heaven which all may enter. The sovereign of the western heaven is Amitabha (or in Chinese O-mi-to-fo), with whom Kuan Yin, the goddess of Mercy, is usually associated. Amitabha is explained as meaning "boundless age." The original meaning is "boundless light," which suggests a Persian origin with Mannichean influences. The translations of the Amitabha sutras were wholly made by natives of central Asia.

Amitabha is one of the thousand Buddhas; he is regarded as the reflex of Sakyamuni and is connected also in his earthly incarnation with a monk called Dharmakara. This monk desired to become a Buddha. This wish he presented to Lokes'vararaja asking him to teach him as to what a Buddha and a Buddha country ought to be. Lokes'vararaja imparted this knowledge. Then the monk after meditation returned having made forty-eight vows that he would not become a Buddha, until all living beings should attain salvation in his heaven.

The eighteenth vow expresses his ideal:

"O Bhagavat, if those beings who have directed their thought towards the highest perfect knowledge in other worlds, and who, after having heard my name, when I have obtained Bodhi (knowledge), have meditated on me with serene thoughts; if at the moment of their death, after having approached them surrounded by an assembly of monks, I should not stand before them worshipped by them, that is, so that their thoughts should not be troubled, then may I not obtain the highest perfect knowledge."

50

A few extracts from the *Amitabha Vyuha Sutra* will illustrate the Buddhist idea of life in this Pure Land:

"In the western region beyond one hundred thousand myriads of Buddhist lands there is a world. Great Happiness by name. This land has a Buddha called Amitabha. The living beings there do not suffer any pain, but enjoy all happiness. Therefore, it is called the land of Pure Delight ... the land of Pure Delight has seven precious fountains full of water containing the eight virtues. The bottom of these fountains is covered with golden sand. On four sides there are steps made of gold, silver, crystal and glass, precious stones, red pearls, and highly polished agates. In the pools are variously colored, light emitting lotus flowers as large as cart wheels, delicate, admirable, odorous and pure..."

"The Buddha of this land makes heavenly music. It is covered with gold. Morning and evening during six hours it rains the wonderful celestial flowers (Erythrina Indica). All the inhabitants of this land on clear mornings after dressing offer these celestial flowers to the hundred thousand myriads of Buddhas of the regions who return to their country at meal time. When they have eaten they go away again."

"This country possesses every kind of wonderful varicolored birds, the white egret, the peacock, the parrot, the s'rarika (a long legged bird), the Kalavingka (a sweet voiced bird) ... All these birds, morning and evening during the six hours, utter forth a beautiful harmonious sound. Their song produces the five *indrya* (roots of faith, energy, memory, ecstatic meditation, wisdom), the five *bala* (the powers of faith, energy, memory, meditation and wisdom), the seven *bodhyanga* (the seven degrees of intelligence, memory, discrimination, energy, tranquillity, ecstatic contemplation, indifference), and the eight portions of the correct path *marga*, (the possession of correct views, decision and purity of thought and will, the ability of reproducing any sound uttered in the universe, vow of poverty, asceticism, attainment of meditative abstraction of self-control, religious recollectedness, honesty and virtue), and such doctrines. When all beings of this land have heard the music, they declare their faithfulness to the Buddha, Dharma and the Sangha (the Buddha, the Law and the community of monks)."

As to those who enter this land it says:

"All living beings who hear this should make a vow to be born in that land. How can they reach the Pure Land? All very good men will gather in that place ... He whose blessedness and virtue are great can be born into that country. If there is a good man or woman who, on hearing of Amitabha, takes this name and holds it in his mind one, two, three, four, five, six, or seven days, and his whole heart is not distracted, to that man at death Amitabha will appear. His heart will not be disturbed. He will at once enter into life in the land of Pure Delight of Amitabha. I see this blessing and hence utter these words. Those living beings who hear these words should make a vow to be born in that land."

4. The Harmonization of These Ideas with Ancestor Worship

The extension of life beyond the grave in purgatory, or in the Pure Land and through transmigration was readily accepted in China. Both the new ideas and the disciplines through which to realize them were eagerly adopted, and have held their place to this day. In other lands the creation of a heaven and a hades has weakened the grip of ancestor worship and ultimately displaced it. In China the opposite result has obtained, due, no doubt, to the fact that the family system and along with it the supreme duty of filial piety were fostered by the state and Buddhism and its teachings were permitted only in so far as they bolstered it up. Another reason lies in the agricultural basis of China's civilization, reenforced by the great difficulty of communication, which tended to make the family system dominant in China. Today, the improvement of communication and the introduction of the industrial system of the West with the individual emphasis of modern education are factors which are weakening the family system and with it ancestral worship.

VIII. THE SPIRITUAL VALUES EMPHASIZED BY BUDDHISM IN CHINA

Near the House of Parliament in Peking is located a small monastery dedicated to the goddess of Mercy, Kuan Yin. Before her image the incense burners send forth curling clouds of smoke. The walls are decorated with old paintings of gods and goddesses. The temple with its courtyard has the appearance of prosperity. Its neat reception room, with its tables, chairs and clock, shows the influence of the modern world.

Here a monk in the prime of life spent a few months recently lecturing on Buddhism to members of parliament and to scholars from various parts of China. Frequently the writer used to drop in of an afternoon to discuss Buddhism and its outlook. Usually a simple repast concluded these conversations, the substance of which forms the greater part of this section.

1. The Threefold Classification of Men Under Buddhism

"What does Buddhism do for men?"

"There are in the world at least three classes of men. The lowest class live among material things, they are occupied with possessions. Their life is entangled in the crude and coarse materials which they regard as real. A second, higher class, regard ideas as realities. They are not entangled in the maze of things, but are confused by ideas, ascribing reality to them. The third and highest class are those who by meditation have freed themselves from the thraldom of ideas and can enter the sixteen heavens."

2. Salvation for the Common Man

"What can Buddhism do for the lowest class?"

"For this class Buddhism has the ten prohibitions. Every man has in him ten evils, which must be driven out. Three have to do with evil in the body, namely, not to steal, not to kill, not to commit adultery; four belong to the mouth, lying, exaggeration, abuse, and ambiguous talk; three belong to the mind, covetousness, malice, and unbelief."

"Is not this entirely negative?"

"Yes, but it is necessary, for during the process of eliminating these evil deeds, man acquires patience and equanimity. Buddhism does not stop with the prohibitions. The believer must practice the ten charitable deeds. Not only must he remove the desire to kill living beings, but he must cultivate the desire to save all beings. Not only must he not steal, but he must assist men with his money. Not only must he not give himself to lasciviousness, but he must treat all men with propriety. So each prohibition involves a positive impulse to virtue, which is quite as essential as the refraining from evil."

"What energizing power does Buddhism provide?"

"First, is purgatory with its terrors. The evil man, seeing the consequences of his acts upon himself, becomes afraid to do them and does that which is good. Then there is transmigration with the danger of transmigration into beasts and insects. Again, there are the rewards in the paradise of Amitabha. Moreover, there is even the possibility not only of saving one's self, but by accumulated merit of saving one's parents and relatives and shortening their stay in purgatory."

3. The Place of Faith

"Can any man enter the western paradise of Amitabha?"

"Yes, it is open to all men. The sutra says: 'If there be any one who commits evil deeds, and even completes the ten evil actions, the five deadly sins and the like; that man, being himself stupid and guilty of many crimes, deserves to fall into a miserable path of existence and suffer endless pains during many long ages. On the eve of death he may meet a good and learned teacher who, soothing and encouraging him in various ways, will preach to him the excellent Law and teach him the remembrance of Buddha, but being harassed by pains', he will have no time to think of Buddha.'"

"What hope has such a man?"

"Even such a man has hope. The sutra says: 'Some good friend will say to him: Even if thou canst not exercise the remembrance of Buddha, utter the name of Buddha Amitabha.' Let him do so serenely with his voice uninterrupted; let him be (continually) thinking of Buddha, until he has completed ten times the thought, repeating 'Namah O-mi-to-fo,' I put my trust in Buddha! On the strength of (his merit of) uttering Buddha's name he will, during every repetition expiate the sins which involve him in births and deaths during eighty millions of long ages. He will, while dying, see a golden lotus-flower, like the disk of the sun, appearing before his eyes; in a moment he will be born in the world of highest happiness. After twelve greater ages the lotus-flower will unfold; thereupon the Bodhisattvas, Avalokitesvaras and Mahasattva's, raising

54

their voices in great compassion, will preach to him in detail the real state of all the elements of nature and the law of the expiation of sins."

"Does faith save such a man?"

"Yes, not his own faith, but the faith which prompted the vow of Amitabha. Amitabha's faith in the possibility of his salvation gives him supreme confidence that he will attain salvation. All he needs is to have the desire to be born in that paradise and to repeat the name of Amitabha."

4. Salvation of the Second Class

"How do those of the second class attain salvation?"

"The men of the second class regard ideas as realities. They are not entangled in the maze of things, but are confused by ideas, regarding them as real. These men do not need images and outward sanctions, but they need heaven and purgatory though regarding them as ideas. By performing the ten good deeds they will obtain a quiet heart, having no fear, and become saints and sages. Among men, saints and sages occupy a high rank, but not so among Buddhists. By merit of good works merely they enter the planes of sensuous desire, the six celestial worlds located immediately above the earth."

5. Salvation for the Highest Class

"And the third class?"

"This class has many ranks. There are those who by the practice of meditation (four *dkyanas*) [Footnote: Dhyana means contemplation. In later times under the influence of the idea of transmigration heavens were imagined which corresponded to the degrees of contemplation.] can enter the sixteen heavens conditioned by form. By the practice of the four *arupa-dhyanas* [Footnote: That degree of abstract contemplation from which all sensations are absent.] they enter the four highest heavens free from all sensuous desires and not conditioned by form. These heavens are the anteroom of Nirvana."

"What is the driving power in all this?"

"It is *virya* or energy."

6. Heaven and Purgatory

"Do heaven and purgatory exist?"

"Heaven and purgatory are in the minds and hearts of men. Really heaven is in the mind of Amitabha and purgatory exists in the illusioned brains of men."

"Does anything exist?"

"Nagarjuna says: 'There is no production, no destruction, no annihilation, no persistence, no unity, no plurality, no coming in and no going forth.'"

7. Sin

"Does sin exist?"

"In the mind of the real Buddhist sin and virtue are different aspects of the all. Sin is illusion; virtue is illusion, There is a higher unity in which they are reconciled."

8. Nirvana

"Do you know of any one who attained Nirvana?"

"Yes, I have experienced it. It is not a state beyond the grave. It is a state into which one can enter here."

"Can you express this experience in words?"

"Impossible. I can only indicate the shore of this great ocean. At first I was in great distress and agony, as though carrying the illusions of the world. Then came a great peace and calm, ineffable, serene, and surpassing the power of language to express."

9. The Philosophical Background

"What is behind this universe!"

"Underlying this universe of phenomena and change there is a unity. It is the basis of all being. It is within all being and all being rests in it. It is because of this common background that men are able to apprehend it. This universal basis we call *dharma,* or law. Its characteristics are that everything born grows old, is subject to disease and death; that the teachings of Buddha purify the mind and enable it to obtain supreme enlightenment; that all Buddhas by treading the same way of perfection will attain the highest freedom."

"You speak of the Buddhist Trinity."

"Yes, we have the Dharmakaya. This is the essence-body, the ground of all being, taking many forms, Buddhas, Bodhisattvas, spirits, angels, men and even demons. It is impersonal, all-pervasive. It may be called the first person. The second person is the Sambhogakaya, the body of bliss. This is the heavenly manifestation of Buddha. The third person is the Nirmanakaya. This is the projection of the body of bliss on earth."

Some identify this trinity with that of the Christian faith. While there is a resemblance, we should note that the first person of the Buddhist trinity would correspond to God as the absolute or the impersonal background of universal Being. The second corresponds to the glorified Christ and the third to the historic Jesus. There is no counterpart either to God the Father or to the Holy Spirit.

"Do you believe in the salvation of all beings?"

"Yes, all have the Buddha heart. All living beings will finally become Buddhas."

Then turning to a friend of mine the speaker said: "What have you done in Buddhism?" The friend answered: "I have written and translated many books." "I do not mean that," he answered. "What *work* have you done?" The friend confessed that he had not done much else. Then he said: "Every morning when you awake, reflect deeply and profoundly upon your state before you were born. Think back to that state where your soul was merged with Buddha. Find yourself in that state and you will find ineffable enlightenment and joy."

The sun was setting behind the Western hills. The blare of trumpets sounded on the city wall. Outside of the door was the whirling sound of Peking returning home from its mundane tasks and joys. We joined the rushing, restless crowd and still we felt the calm of another world. Has not Christianity a message of balm and peace for these sons of the East who are so sensitive to the touch of the eternal and sublime?

10. What Buddhism Has to Give

An important government official obliged to deal with many vexatious requests and demands declared: "I could not get through my day's work, if I did not spend an hour every day in meditation, just as Buddha did when he became enlightened." He was asked what he did when he meditated or prayed. "Nothing at all." "Well, about what do you think?" "Of nothing at all. I stop thinking when I engage in religious meditation. Life makes me think too much. I should lose my sanity, if I did not stop thinking and enter into the 'void', whence we all came and into which we all are going to drop back."

His Christian inquirer still was unsatisfied by the Buddhist's description of his prayer life, and pressed further for details. "What happens when you meditate or pray?"

"Nothing happens, I tell you, except, that I experience a peace which the passing world cannot give and which the passing world cannot altogether take away. The secret of religion is simply to realize that everything is passing away. When you accept that fact, then you become really free. The Christian world seemed to have been tremendously impressed by the slogan of the French soldiers at Verdun, 'They shall not pass!' Perhaps the German soldiers did not pass just then or there. But the French soldiers themselves are all passing away. And everything in the world is passing away. What our Buddhist religion teaches us is: 'Let it pass!' You cannot keep anything for very long. And prayer or meditation is simply to practice yourself in that thought deliberately. Oh, it is a wonderful peace when you fully believe that gospel, and enter into it every day. Vanity of vanities, everything is vanity! Why worry? We do altogether too much worrying. To pray means simply to quit worrying, to quit thinking, to enter into the indescribably passionless peace of Nirvana."

Here seemed to be an ardent Buddhist. When asked what he thought as the difference between a Buddhist and a Christian, he answered promptly:

"Yes, there is my wife. She is a very good woman. All the neighbors come to her, when there is any one sick or in trouble. So I say to her: 'Wife, I should think you would make a first-class Christian.' But I think she lets herself be worried by altogether too many troubles. She is all the time thinking and fussing and planning. To be sure, it is mostly about other people, But then she does have the children and the house and the relatives and friends and neighbors to look after. Perhaps she really cannot be a Buddhist. Perhaps it is all a matter of temperament. Oh, but I tell you it is great to be a Buddhist, because it gives you such a wonderful peace."

IX. PRESENT-DAY BUDDHISM:

1. Periods of Buddhist History

The history of Buddhism in China may be divided into four periods. Buddhism entered China, as we have seen, in the second century B.C. The first period, that of the translation and propagation of the faith, ended in 420 A.D. The second period, that of interpenetration, lasted to the beginning of the T'ang dynasty, 618 A.D. The third, the period of establishment, ended with the close of the five dynasties, in 960 A.D. The fourth period, that of decay, has extended to the present day.

2. The Progress of the Last Twenty-five Years

There are signs of a revival of Buddhism in China. Whether this is a tide, or a wave, only the future can reveal. In 1893 Dharmapala, an Indian monk, stopped in Shanghai on his way back from the Congress of Religions in Chicago. It was his purpose to make a tour of China, to arouse the Chinese Buddhists to send missionaries to India to restore Buddhism there, and then to start a propaganda throughout the whole world. He addressed the monks of Shanghai. Dr. Edkins, the veteran missionary, acted as his interpreter. Dharmapala was surrounded by a horde of curious monks who were more interested in his strange appearance and in the cost of his garments than they were in his great ideals. They were also feeling the iron heel of the Confucian government and at once inquired about the attitude of the government toward such an innovation. Dharmapala did not go beyond Shanghai.

Japanese Buddhists, especially the members of the Hongwanji sect, have taken a deep interest in Chinese Buddhists. Count Otani once visited the chief monasteries of China. Numerous Japanese Buddhists have made such visits. In 1902, the Empress Dowager, fired by a reforming zeal, decided to confiscate Buddhist property and to use the proceeds for the spread of modern education. The Buddhist monasteries put themselves under the protection of Japanese monks in order to hold their property. When by 1906 the Empress Dowager saw the consequences of her edict, she at once issued a new edict, reversing the former one, and the Japanese monks took their departure.

The Japanese Buddhists have been fired by missionary zeal for China. In many of the large cities of China are the temples of the Hongwanji sect. Established primarily for the Japanese, these temples are intended to serve as points of departure for a nation-wide missionary work. The twenty-one demands made upon China included two significant items in the last group which the Chinese refused to sign: "Art. 2: Japanese hospitals, churches and schools in the interior of China shall be granted the right of owning land." "Art. 7: China agrees that Japanese subjects shall have the right of missionary propaganda in China."

Under Japanese influence there was established in 1907 at Nanking, under the leadership of Yang, a lay Buddhist devotee, a school for the training of Buddhist missionaries. The students were to go to Japan for further training, and the more promising ones were to study in India. This project was discontinued after the death of Yang on account of the lack of funds.

When the republic was established Buddhism felt a wave of reform. The monasteries established schools for monks and children. A magazine was published which appeared irregularly for several numbers and then stopped. A national organization was formed with headquarters at Peking. A survey of monasteries was begun. The activities in lecturing and propaganda were increased, but Yuan Shih-kai issued twenty-seven regulations for the control of Buddhist monasteries, which markedly dampened the ardor of the reformers.

The world war which accentuated the spirit of nationalism had the added effect of stirring up Buddhist enthusiasm. There are at present signs of new activity among them in China.

3. Present Activities

While Buddhism may be standing still or even dying in certain parts of China, it is showing signs of new life in the provinces of Kiangsu and Chekiang and in the large cities. Such revival in centers subject to the influence of the modern world shows that Buddhism in China as in Japan has sufficient vitality to adjust itself to modern conditions. Let us consider some of these activities.

(a) The Reconstruction of Monasteries.—During the T'ai Ping rebellion, which devastated China in 1850-1865, the monasteries suffered with the towns. Not only were the monasteries burned to the ground, but their means of support were taken away and the monks were scattered. There are still many of these ruined monasteries in the Yangtze valley and in southern and western China. Quite a number of them have been rebuilt. Perhaps the most notable example is that at Changchow which was destroyed during the rebellion. Today it is the largest monastery in China, having about two thousand monks. In Fukien several new monasteries have been built in the last few decades. In the provinces of Chekiang and Kiangsu, in the large cities and about Peking there are building activities, showing that the monasteries are feeling a new wave of prosperity.

T'ai Hsu, one of the leaders' of modern Buddhism, is holding up an ideal program for Buddhism in this time of reconstruction. He proposes that there should be 576 central monasteries, 4608 preaching places, 72 Buddhist hospitals and 72 orphanages.

(b) Accessions.—Regarding the number of monks it is almost impossible to obtain any reliable figures. A conservative estimate, based upon partial returns, makes the number of monks about 400,000 and that of nuns about 10,000. The impression among the Buddhists is that the number of monks is increasing. That is quite probable in view of the rebuilding and repairing which is now in progress.

More significant is the number of accessions from the learned class. Many officials, disheartened by the present confused political situation, have sought refuge in the monasteries. Some of them are now abbots of monasteries and are using their influence to build them up. All over China there are Confucian scholars who are giving themselves to the study of Buddhism and to meditation. Some of the Chinese students who have studied in Buddhist universities in Japan are propagating Buddhism by lecture and pen.

(c) Publications.—Quite as significant is the increase in the publication of Buddhist literature of all kinds. Many of the monasteries have printing departments where they publish the sutras needed for their own use. In addition, there are eight or more publishing centers where Buddhist literature is printed. The most famous are Yang's establishment at Nanking, the Buddhist Press in Yangchow and that in Peking. In these establishments about nine hundred different works are being published. The most noteworthy recent publication has been that of the Chinese Buddhist Tripitaka in Shanghai.

Among these publications are a few modern issues. The Chung Hua Book Company has published several works on Buddhism. Other books have been issued for the sake of harmonizing Buddhism with western science and philosophy. In this enterprise Japanese influence is visible. In 1921 a Shanghai press published a dictionary of Buddhist terms containing 3302 pages, based on the Japanese Dictionary of Buddhism. Other works also show the influence of Japanese scholarship.

Among the publications have appeared two magazines. One published at Ningpo, is called "New Buddhism." This is struggling and may have to succumb. The other is known as the "Sound of the Sea Tide," now published in Hankow. Moreover, in all the large cities there are Buddhist bookshops where only Buddhist works are sold. These all report a good business. This literary activity reveals an interest among the reading classes of China. Few such books are purchased by the monks. The Chinese scholars read them for their style and for their deep philosophy, but also for light and for help in the present distracting political situation of their country.

(d) Lectures.—Along with publication goes the spread of Buddhism by lectures in the monasteries and the cities of China. A few years ago Buddhist sermons, however serious, were only listened to by monks and by a few pious devotees. Today such addresses are advertised and are usually well attended by the intellectuals. Often many women are found listening. Monks like T'ai Hsue and Yuan Ying have a national reputation. Not only monks, but laymen trained in Japan are delivering lectures on the Buddhist sutras. The favorites are the Awakening of Faith and the Suddharma Pundarika sutra.

(e) Buddhist Societies.—With the lectures goes the organization of Buddhist societies for all sorts of purposes. There is a central society in Peking which has branches in every province. The connection is rather loose. Buddhism has never been in favor of centralization. Nor for that matter would the government have allowed it. The chief ends aimed at by these societies are fellowship, devotion, study, propagation, and service. Such societies, often short lived, are springing up in many quarters. They meet for lectures on Buddhism or to conduct a study class in some of the sutras. Occasionally the more ambitious conduct an institute for several months. Some spend part of the time in meditation together. Several schools for children are supported by these societies. They also encourage work of a religious nature among prisoners, distributing tracts and holding services. Such activities are especially appreciated by those who are to suffer the death penalty. The societies are also doing publishing work. The two magazines are supported by the members of the larger societies.

(f) Signs of Social Ambition.—Social work is a prominent feature of some of these Buddhist societies. They have raised money for famine stricken regions, have opened orphanages, and assist in Red Cross work. One of the largest Chinese institutions for ministering to people who are sick and in trouble is located at Hankow. Around a central Buddhist temple is a modern-built hospital, an orphanage and several schools for poor children. It may not maintain western standards of efficiency, but it certainly represents the outreach of modern Buddhism.

Perhaps their most far-reaching advance has been made because of the realization that leaders are needed and that they must be trained. Several schools for this purpose have sprung into existence. Such schools are necessarily very primitive and are struggling with the difficulties of finding an adequate staff and equipment and of obtaining the best type of students.

Another sign of new life has been the making of programs for the future development of Buddhism. One of the most comprehensive appeared a short time ago. For the individual it proposes the cultivation of love, mercy, equality, freedom, progressiveness, an established faith, patience and endurance. For all men it proposes (1) an education according to capacity; (2) a trade suited to ability; (3) an opportunity to develop one's powers; (4) a chance for enlightenment for all. For society it urges the cultivation of cooperation, social service, sacrifice for the social weal, and the social consciousness in the individual. On behalf of the country it urges patriotism, participation in the government, and cooperation in international movements. For the world it advocates universal progress. As to the universe it specifies as a goal the bringing of men into harmony with spiritual realities, the enlightenment of all and the realization of the spiritual universe.

A Buddhist writer sums up the aims of new Buddhism as follows:

"Formerly Buddhism desired to escape the sinful world. Today Buddhism not only desires to escape this world of sin, but longs to transform this world of sin into a new world dominated by the ideals of Buddhism. Formerly Buddhism was occupied with erecting and perfecting its doctrines and polity as an organization. Today it not only hopes to perfect the doctrines and polity, but desires to spread the doctrines and ideals abroad so as to help mankind to become truly cultured."

4. The Attitude of Tibetan Lamas

Not only the Chinese Buddhists, but the Lamas of Mongolia and Tibet are feeling the impulses of the new age. Quite recently an exhibition was held in the Lama temple at Peking which attracted thousands of visitors. Its object was to obtain money to repair the temple, and thus to give its work a fresh impulse. That these impulses are not necessarily hostile to Christianity is shown by a letter written by the Kurung Tsering Lama of Kokonor district to the Rev. T. Soerensen of Szechuan:

"I, your humble servant, have seen several copies of the Scriptures and, having read them carefully, they certainly made me believe in Christ. I understand a little of the outstanding principles and the doctrinal teaching of the One Son, but as to the Holy Spirit's nature and essence, and as to the origin of this religion, I am not at all clear, and it is therefore important that the doctrinal principles of this religion should be fully explained, so as to enlighten the unintelligent and people of small mental ability.

"The teaching of the science of medicine and astrology is also very important. It is therefore evident if we want this blessing openly manifested, we must believe in the religion of the only Son of God. Being in earnest, I therefore pray you from my heart not to consider this letter lightly. With a hundred salutations."

Enclosed with this letter was a poem written in most elegant language.

"O thou Supreme God and most precious Father, The truth above all religions, The Ruler of all animate and inanimate worlds! Greater than wisdom, separated from birth and death, Is his son Christ the Lord shining in glory among endless beings. Incomprehensible wonder, miraculously made! In this teaching I myself also believe—As your spirit is with heaven united, My soul undivided is seeking the truth Jesus the Savior's desire fulfilling, For the coming of the Kingdom of Heaven I am praying. Happiness to all."

5. The Buddhist World Versus the Christian World

Looking back over the last twenty-five years we see rising quite distinctly a Buddhist world growing conscious of itself, of its past history and of its mission to the world. This Buddhist, world has much more of a program than it had twenty-five years ago. Its object is to unite the Mahayana and the Hinayana branches of Buddhism and to spread Buddhist propaganda over the world. At present the leadership of this movement is in Japan. It is in part a political movement. There is no question that Christianity is not at all pleasing to the Japanese militarists. It is regarded by them as the advance post of western industrialism and political ambition. Quite naturally such leaders desire to make the Buddhist world a unit. It is also a social movement. The spirit of the Japanese Buddhist has been brought to consciousness by the new position of Japan. Japan is seeking to take its place in the world as a first rate power. By this not only will Japan's industry and commerce profit, but its spiritual values must also be adapted to the world. The movement then has its spiritual side. Japanese travelers and people are going to all parts of the world. They carry with them the religious ideals which have been shaped by Buddhism. Buddhism in the past was one of the great religions of salvation with an inspiring missionary message. It is again awakening to this task of evangelization. Under the leadership of Japanese scholars and religious statesmen the Japanese are seeking to unite the Buddhist world so that it shall become a force in the new world. Japan is thus trying to give back what it has received in the past.

At present in Buddhist countries there is a strong force working against this movement. Nationalism is a new force to be reckoned with. Still even with the spirit of nationalism permeating every group, the Buddhist world is getting together and will strive to make its contribution to the life of the whole world.

X. THE CHRISTIAN APPROACH TO BUDDHISTS

1. Questions Which Buddhists Ask

Buddhists are approaching Christianity. In many places a spirit of inquiry and interest in the Christian religion is met. It is not necessary that there should be a Buddhist world permanently over against a Christian world. The questions which Buddhists ask a missionary indicate an interest in vital themes. Some of them are as follows:

We put our trust in the three Precious Ones. In what do you trust? Is not your Shang Ti (name for God used in China) a being lower than Buddha and just a little higher than a Bodhisattva? Is not Shang Ti the tribal god of the Jews? Do you believe in the existence of *purgatory?* What sufferings will those endure who do not live a virtuous life? Do you believe in the reality of the Western Paradise? How can one enter it? There being three kinds of merit, by what method is the great merit accumulated? How is the middle and the small merit accumulated? What are the fruits of these proportions of merit and what are they like? Tell me how to believe Christ. What work of meditation do you perform? Is not Buddhism more democratic than Christianity, because it holds out the possibility of Buddhahood to all beings? Is not Buddhism more inclusive, because it provides for the salvation of all beings?

2. Knowledge and Sympathy

These questions make it plain that the worker who is to deal with Buddhists should have a broad background of general culture. He must be thoroughly humanized. He should have a good knowledge of the history of philosophy and religion, including the work of the modern philosophers. A knowledge of the life of Buddha and of the doctrines of the Hinayana or Southern Buddhism, as well as the tenets of the Mahayana should be in his possession. The psychology of religion should interpenetrate his historical learning; the best methods of pedagogy should guide his approach to men. Of course he must speak the language of the Buddhist, not only the spiritual language, but his everyday patois. He will find it an advantage to know some Sanskrit. While this requirement is not very urgent at present, it will rapidly become a necessity for doing the best work.

This knowledge should be interpenetrated by a genuine sympathy, that is, imagination tinged with emotion. The worker should be able to view doctrines, values and actions from the point of view of the Buddhist and his past history. He must have a genuine interest in and a great capacity for friendship. The Buddhists are very human, responding to friendship very quickly. Such friendship forms a link between the man and the larger friendship of Christ.

3. Emphasis on the Aesthetic in Christianity

A Chinese Christian leader described his idea of a church as a place removed from the din of the street, approached by a walk flanked with trees and flowers and adorned within by symbols speaking to the heart of the Chinese. He longed for the mystic silence and the beauty of holiness which would open the windows of the world of spiritual reality and throw its light upon the problems of life. He was asked, "Would you adapt some of the symbols of the Chinese religions?" He said, "Many of those symbols are neutral. They suggest religious emotion. Their character depends upon the content which the occasion puts into them. If the content is Christian then the symbols and emotions will become Christian."

Christianity is a religion of beauty. The beautiful in architecture, symbol and ritual, expressing the spiritual universe of the past, present and future, makes a strong appeal to the Chinese heart. It may well be emphasized in the future as never before.

4. Emphasis on the Mystical in Christianity

Not long ago a Buddhist in one of the large cities of China was converted. He found great joy in the experience which revived him and gathered into unity the broken fragments of his life. He attended church regularly and participated in the prayer meetings. Gradually he discovered that he was not being nourished. He felt his joy slipping away from him and his divided life reinstating itself. He went to Buddhism for consolation. He is not hostile to the church. He appreciates the help he received, but he said that he came for consolation and peace and found the same—hard orthodoxy and morality so familiar to him in Confucianism.

While the case of this man may have individual peculiarities, it may be made the starting point for a discussion of the situation in many churches in China. The early message to the Chinese was doctrinal. The false notion of many gods had to be displaced by the idea of the one true God. With this idea of the true God a few other tenets of the Christian religion are often held as dogmatic propositions to be repeated when questions are asked. The great sin preached is the worship of idols.

The second part of the Christian message is salvation by faith in Jesus Christ. This salvation is other-worldly to a large extent. The extreme emphasis upon it has made of the church an insurance society, membership in which insures bliss in the world beyond.

The third part of the message has been concerned with moral acts, abstinence from opium (liquor and tobacco in some churches), polygamy, and the gross sins. Attendance upon church services, contribution for the support of the church, and the refusal to contribute to idolatry have also been required.

The emphasis to a large extent was doctrinal, moral and individual. The result has been a body of people free from the gross sins, but also innocent of the great virtues and individualistic in their outlook upon this world and the next. This emphasis is needed, but in addition there should be the cultivation of the presence of God in the soul by appropriate means. The Christian Church of China should develop a technique of the spiritual life suited to the East. The formation of habits of devotion should be emphasized. Intercessory prayer should be given a larger place. Contemplation and meditation should be regarded not merely as an escape from the turmoil and strife of the world, but as a preparation for the highest life of service and sacrifice. Buddhist mysticism united the whole universe and was the great foundation of Chinese art, literature and morality. The spiritual world of Christianity must likewise seep through into the very thought of Asia and inspire the new art, literature and morality which will be the world expression of a Christian universe.

5. Emphasis on the Social Elements in Christianity

To the aesthetic and mystical emphasis must be attached a social emphasis. Buddhism is often criticized as not being social. It is a highly socialized religion. It has had a large influence upon social life in the East. This social life is different from ours. We see its wrongs and weaknesses. Likewise do the Buddhists see the materialism and injustice of our social life. Christianity must relate itself to the modern world as it is rising in China and seek not merely to remedy a few wrongs or heal a few diseases, but must release the healing stream into the social life of the East. This will be done and is being done through the Church community which has become conscious of itself, realizing its needs and wants, seeking in an intelligent and systematic way to rehabilitate itself. It is not so much the external unrelated efforts that accomplish the thing needed, but it is rather the community life stirred by ideals and fired by a new dynamic which begins the work of reformation.

6. Emphasis on the Person of Jesus Christ

(a) As a Historical Character.—The great asset of the missionary among Buddhists is the historical person of Christ. In contrast to many of the Bodhisattvas, the saviours of the Buddhists, Jesus is a historical character. His life among men was the life of God among men.

(b) As the Revealer.—God is like Christ. Christ reveals God as the complete, the perfect person. He possessed the pure spiritual personality. The chief characteristic of this personality is love. This love conscious of itself finds its highest joy in the well-being of others. This love of God produced human life which, springing from the lowest form, broke through the material elements and is capable of attaining the highest development.

Christ reveals to man his heavenly relationship. Man created in the likeness of God stands in the highest relation of one person to another through love. He likens this relation to that of father and son. He lifts man to the fellowship with the divine. Yet such a fellowship that man preserves his personality.

Christ reveals man in his relation to men as a brother and the form of love which shall control the relation of man to God as well as man to man.

Christ revealed and founded the Kingdom, a society of the saved, dominated by the spirit of the founder and making this spirit of love and service the organizing power in the world.

(c) As the Saviour.—Mahayana Buddhism emphasized saviourhood. Christ is the saviour of men. In Buddhism the stress is placed upon the merit of the saviour and the saved. There is no question that merit has some value. Yet Christ does not save us by merit, nor do we help to save one another by merit. Salvation is a moral and spiritual process. It is concerned with the biology of the soul. The salvation that we preach is not the salvation by knowledge, or meditation, or merit, but by the interpenetration of Christ's spirit in ours, by the mystic and moral union of our life with his. As Paul says: "That I may know Him and the power of His resurrection and the fellowship of His suffering." Yet He is not the saviour of the individual alone. He saves the community, the church. Only as His spirit permeates and dominates the community does he find his true self and the real salvation.

(d) As the Eternal Son, of God.—The Mahayana system does not emphasize the historicity of Amitabha or of the Bodhisattvas. Spiritual truth is the development of the soul. It is not limited by time and place. Likewise Christianity must emphasize the eternal character of Jesus Christ. "The Logos existed in the very beginning, the Logos was with God, the Logos was God." To the Mahayanist this spiritual history is more real than any fact conditioned by time and place.

The Christian worker must learn to understand the import of the Gospel of John. He must see in Jesus Christ "The real Light, which enlightens every man." He must be able to convince himself that the Christ is the fulfillment of the highest aspirations of the Mahayana system.

7. How Christianity Expresses Itself in Buddhist Minds

In 1920 a number of Buddhist monks, under the leadership of Rev. K. L. Reichelt formed a Christian brotherhood. The members of this small brotherhood decided that they must subscribe to vows and they took the four following:

"I promise before the Almighty and Omniscient God, that I with my whole heart will surrender myself to the true Trinity, God the Father, the Son and the Holy Spirit. I will with my whole heart have faith in Jesus Christ as the Saviour of the world who gives completion to the profoundest and best objects of the higher Buddhism. I will live in this faith now and ever after.

"I promise solemnly before God with my whole heart to devote myself to the study of the true doctrine and break wholly with the evil manners of the world and show forth in my public and private life that I am truly united with Christ.

"I promise that I in every respect will try so to educate myself that I can be of use in the work of God on earth. I will with undivided heart devote myself to the great work; to lead my brethren in the Buddhist Association forward to the understanding of Christ as the only One, who gives completion to the highest and profoundest ideas of Higher Buddhism.

"I promise that until my last hour I will work so that out of our Christian Brotherhood there may grow forth a strong church of Christ among Buddhists. I will not permit any evil thing to grow in my heart, which could divide the brotherhood, but will always try to promote the progress of every member in the knowledge of the holy obligations laid down in these vows and our constitution."

Such men ought, to make choice Christians.

8. Christianity's Constructive Values

Buddhism in the course of its long history developed certain religious ideas and values which we find in Christianity. It faced the fact of sin and placed it in the heart. It diagnosed the fundamental instincts of men, sex-appetite, will-to-achieve, and pugnacity. These must be overcome. It regards them as delusions which must be eliminated.

69

Christianity also deals with these instincts. It is under no delusion as to their strength. There are certain tendencies in Christianity which have tried to annihilate them. The central tendency of Christianity, however, recognizing their power for good, seeks to sublimate them and make them serve the individual and society. This attitude of the two religions toward these instincts is fundamentally different. The attitude of Christianity has been justified even in Buddhist lands where the religious life of the people has followed the same line that Christianity advocates.

Early Buddhism tried to dissolve man's personality. Later Buddhism corrected this and perhaps has appealed too much to the desire on the part of the individual to enter a heaven which is merely a replica of the earth. Christianity starts with a personal God and holds up before the believer the goal of perfection for his own personality. It finds man without a self and confers a real selfhood upon him.

Early Buddhism taught that salvation is accomplished by the individual alone. It denies the possibility and the necessity of help from a divine source. Subsequent history has proved this to have been wrong. In India, Buddhism has been displaced by Hinduism, and in China, and Japan, the Mahayana has developed the idea of salvation through another. The great stream of Buddhism has recognized that man by himself is helpless. He must have the help of a divine power in order to obtain salvation. Christianity asserts that salvation is possible only through the intervention of God. The incarnation, the life, death and resurrection of Jesus and his work in the world through the Holy Spirit on the one hand are the expression of God's solicitude for man, and, on the other hand, correspond to the deep need which men of all ages have felt, for a power above themselves. From the early stages of magic to the highest reaches of religion we find this constant factor recognized by human groups all over the world. They bear witness to a power above themselves to whom they continually appeal. In Christianity we find this main tendency enunciated most clearly. The individual cannot save himself. Mankind cannot save itself. Both must rely upon the assistance of the divine power which started this universe on its way and which is the ever present creative force.

Christianity, moreover, has established the community of believers including all classes and conditions of men. Herein each one may realize him Herein also he may realize the kind of community which is friendly to his highest aspirations for himself. Herein he has the opportunity to transmute the instincts above mentioned into forces which make for the larger development of his own person and the well-being of the community.

Accordingly, as Christians face Buddhists, they can do so with the consciousness that this great religion has been reaching out after the light which shines brightly in our Christian religion. They have the assurance not only that they have a message which brings fulfilment to the ideas of the Mahayana, but also that it has prepared the way for the hearts of the Chinese to receive the highest message of Christianity.

APPENDIX I. HINTS FOR THE PRELIMINARY STUDY OF BUDDHISM IN CHINA

The student should read and inwardly digest the booklet of K. J. Saunders

He should follow the directions given in Appendix One of that book, This procedure is important because the Hinayana Buddhism and the life of Buddha are the background of Buddhism in China.

Then he may take Hackmann's *Buddhism as a Religion* (No. 15). This will give a general orientation. This may be followed with R. F. Johnston's *Buddhist China* (No. *20*). Along with this he may read Suzuki's *Awakening of Faith* (No. 32), and also his *Outlines of Mahayana Buddhism (No.* 33). McGovern's *Introduction to Mahayana Buddhism* (No. 23) will illuminate the philosophical background of Buddhism, and Eliot's *Hinduism and Buddhism* (No. 13) will add historical perspective.

The translation of *Mahdydna Sutras* by Beal and in the Sacred Books of the East will give him some of the sources for the doctrines held in China. He may begin as the Buddhist missionaries did with the sutra of the Forty-two sections and then take up the Diamond Sutra, and then completing the sutras in Vol. 59 and the Catena of Buddhist Scriptures.

For the study of the ethical side he will find De Groot's *Le Code du Mahayana en Chine* very helpful. For the study of the sects Eliot, Vol. III, pp. 303-320 Northern Buddhism (No. 14) will be helpful.

In all his study he will find Eitel's *Handbook of Chinese Buddhism* (No. 12) indispensable. He must, however, make a Chinese index in order to be able to use the book.

Contact with monks will be helpful and is quite necessary in order to appreciate the human problems of the work.

APPENDIX II. A BRIEF BIBLIOGRAPHY

1. BEAL, S. Abstract of Four Lectures upon Buddhist Literature in China. London, Triibner, 1882.

Lecture II, on "Method of Buddha's Teaching in the Vinaya Pitaka," and Lecture IV, on "Coincidences Between Buddhism and Other Religions," especially desirable.

2. ——*Buddhism in China,* London, S. P. C. K, 1884.

The best comprehensive account of Chinese Buddhism, written by an authority.

3. ——*Catena of Buddhist Scriptures,* from the Chinese. London, Triibner, 1871.

A good introduction to Chinese Buddhism from the sources.

4. ——The Romantic Legend of Sakya Buddha. London, Triibner, 1875.

Recounts Buddha's history from the beginning to the conversion of the Kasyapas and others.

5. ——*Texts from the Buddhist Canon Commonly Known* as D hammapada. London, Triibner, 1878. Pocket edition, 1902.

These "Scriptural Texts," translated from the Chinese and abridged, are usually connected with some event in Buddha's history. This translation has Indian anecdotes, illustrating the verses.

6. COULING, S., editor. *The Encyclopaedia Sinica.* Shanghai, Kelly &Walsh, 1917.

Contains, on pages 67-75, a number of brief articles upon Buddhism in China.

7. DE QROOT, J. J. M. *Religion of the Chinese.* New York, Macmillan, 1900.

Pages 164-223 contain a summary of the main facts about Chinese Buddhism by an authority.

8. ——Sectarianism and Religious Persecution in China. 2 vols. J. Mueller, Amsterdam, 1903-1904.

Treats from sources Confucianism's persecution of Buddhism and other sects. See Vol. II. Index, under Buddhism, p. 572.

9. DORE, HENEI. *Researches into Chinese Superstitions.* 6 vols. Tusewei Press, 1914-1920.

A well illustrated miscellany of superstitions of all Chinese religions showing indistinctly their interpenetration by Buddhism. For Buddhism proper, see Vol. VI, pp. 89-233.

10. EDKINS, J. *Chinese Buddhism.* 2d edition. London, Truebner, 1893.

A very full account of Buddhism as seen by a Sinologue of the last generation.

11. EITEL, E. J. Buddhism: Its Historical, Theoretical and Popular Aspects. Hongkong, Lane, Crawford and Co., 1884.

Written by an observant scholar and descriptive of Buddhism of South China especially.

12. ——*Handbook of Chinese Buddhism.* Presbyterian Mission Press, Shanghai.

This is a Sanskrit-Chinese dictionary, a reprint of the second edition of 1888 without the Chinese index necessary for identifying Chinese Buddhist terms.

13. ELIOT, SIR CHARLES. *Hinduism and Buddhism, An Historical Sketch.* 3 vols. Edward Arnold and Co., 1921.

This is a valuable contribution to our knowledge of Buddhism by an experienced student. The parts especially related to Chinese Buddhism are Vol. II, pp. 3-106; Vol. III, 223-335.

14. JETTY, A. *Gods of Northern Buddhism.* Oxford, Clarendon Press, 1914.

This work is helpful in identifying images in the temples, though unfortunately few of those given are Chinese.

15. HACKMANN, H. *Buddhism as a Religion.* London, Probsthain, 1910.

Gives a general view of Buddhism from first-hand investigation. For Chinese Buddhism see pp. 200-257.

16. HASTINGS, JAMES. *The Encyclopedia of Religion and Ethics.* New York, Scribners, 1908.

Articles Asvaghosa, Bodhisattva, China (Buddhism in), Mahayana Missions (Buddhist).

17. HUME, R. E. *The Living Religions of the World.* New York, Scribners, 1924.

A clear comparative study of these religions in the light of Christian standards.

18. INGLIS, J. W. "Christian Element in Chinese Buddhism." *International Review of Missions,* Vol. V, 1916, pp. 587-602. An excellent article by a veteran missionary and scholar of Manchuria.

19. JOHNSON, S. *Oriental Religions ... China.* Boston, Houghton, Osgood Co., 1878.

Pages 800-833 give a comprehensive summary by a student of comparative religion.

20. JOHNSTON, R. F. *Buddhist* China. New York, Dutton, 1913.

A well-written, interesting book. The author knows his subject, and is held in high esteem by Buddhists in China.

21. KEITH, A. BERRIEDALE. *Buddhist Philosophy in India and Ceylon.* Oxford, Clarendon Press, 1923.

A study of the historic development of the Buddhistic philosophy in India and Ceylon which throws much light on the Mahayana.

22. LODGE, J. E. *Chinese Buddhist Art.* Asia, Vol. XIX, June, 1919.

Some of the choicest half-tones illustrating its character accompanied by interesting descriptions.

23. McGOVERN, W. M. An Introduction of Mahayana Buddhism. Dutton, 1922.

Though written from the point of view of Japanese Buddhism it gives a good treatment of metaphysical and psychological aspects of the Mahayana system.

24. MUeLLER, F. MAX. *Sacred Books of the East.* Vol. XLIX, Buddhist, Mahayana Texts. Oxford, Clarendon Press, 1894.

A book of sources necessary for understanding Northern Buddhism.

25. PARKER, E. H. *China and Religion.* New York, Dutton, 1905.

A sketch of Buddhism by a scholar long resident in China is found in Chapter IV.

26. PAUL, C. T. *The Presentation of Christianity to Buddhists.* New York, Board of Missionary Preparation, 1924.

A carefully prepared study of Buddhism from the viewpoint of missionaries working in Buddhist lands.

27. REICHELT, K. L. "Special Work Among Chinese Buddhists." *Chinese Recorder,* Vol. LI, 1920, July issue, pp. 491-497.

An article by a pioneer in work among Buddhists, of rare insight and sympathy.

28. RICHARD, T. The Awakening of Faith in the Mahayana Doctrine. 2d edition. Shanghai, 1918.

A loose translation by a very large-hearted and sympathetic student with an irenic spirit. See 32 below.

29. RICHARD, T. *Guide to Buddhahood; Being a Standard Manual of Chinese Buddhism.* Shanghai., 1907.

30. SAUNDERS, K. J. *Epochs of Buddhist History* (Haskell Lectures), Chicago University Press, 1922.

A good summary of the main developments in Buddhism.

31. STAUFFER, M. T. *The Christian Occupation of China.* Shanghai Continuation Committee, 1922.

The introductory section contains articles upon China's religions.

32. SUZUKI, T. A'svaghosa's *Awakening of Faith in the Mahayana.* Chicago, Open Court Publishing Co., 1900.

A far more accurate translation of this work than No. 28 above.

33. ――Outlines of *Mahayana Buddhism.* Chicago, Open Court Publishing Co., 1908.

While written from the Japanese point of view it is necessary to the understanding of Chinese Buddhism.

34. WATTERS, T. "Buddhism in China." *Chinese Recorder,* Vol. II, 1870, pp. 1-7, 38-43, 64-68, 81-88, 117-122, 145-150, Shanghai.

A valuable series of articles by an excellent Chinese scholar, discussing the history, persecutions, and various Buddhas of China.

35. WEI, F. C. M. "Salvation by Faith as Taught by the Pure Land Sect." *Chinese Recorder,* Vol. LI, 1920, pp. 395-401, 485-491.

A good article on the sect whose ideas have spread over China and Japan.

36. WIEGER, L. *Bouddhisme Chinois,* 2 vols. Ho-Kien-Fou, Roman Catholic Press, 1910-1913.